Wicket Keepers
of the
World

Allsport Photographic

Gordon's Gin Wicket-Keepers of the World

Godfrey Evans

Introduction by Trevor Bailey

NEW ENGLISH LIBRARY

Copyright © 1984 by Godfrey Evans

First published in Great Britain in 1984 by New English Library,
Mill Road, Dunton Green, Sevenoaks, Kent.
Editorial office: 47 Bedford Square, London WC1B 3DP

Photoset by Rowland Phototypesetting Ltd,
Bury St Edmunds, Suffolk.

Printed in Great Britain by St Edmundsbury Press,
Bury St Edmunds, Suffolk.

British Library Cataloguing in Publication Data

Evans, Godfrey, *1920–*
   Wicket keepers of the world.
   1. Cricket—Wicket-keeping—History
   —20th century
   I. Title
   796.35'824'09   GV927.5.W53

   ISBN 0 450 06060 8

Contents

Foreword

by J. R. C. Holbech

It is little more than two years since Gordon's Gin entered the world of cricket. Anxious to make a distinctive and valuable contribution to the game, we chose the all-too-often neglected art of wicket-keeping and one of cricket's most remarkable personalities, Godfrey Evans, as our partners. And it's been a successful marriage.

Our Wicket-Keeper Awards have already become a valued and respected part of the cricket scene and have given Godfrey the opportunity to continue to enrich the sport he loves.

We are delighted to be supporting Godfrey's fascinating new book which, typical of the man himself, is a colourful and honest look at the world of wicket-keeping.

Chairman, Gordon's Gin

Preface

It is obvious to me and I am sure to you all, that for me to write a book on Wicket-Keepers of the World I must have had some outside help in compiling what I believe is an important and interesting volume.

To all these people I say a tremendous thank-you, but I must in this acknowledgement single out certain individuals.

My PR friends at Counsel Limited have been marvellous colleagues in the setting-up and running of the Gordon's Gin Wicket-Keeper Awards and have given me enthusiastic support whilst writing this book. They love their work, the game of cricket – and even the occasional gin and tonic.

I am also indebted to John Hughes, Roy Mantle, Frank Nicklin and John Etheridge for their tremendous input during this arduous but very pleasant task; also to Reg Hayter who introduced me to Tony Vinter.

Tony, who has worked in Fleet Street, has written articles for *Wisden* magazine, and did a three-year broadcasting stint for RTE, has a great sense of humour; this, coupled with his enormous enthusiasm for the game, and his ever vigilant mind working to put me back on course whenever I strayed out of orbit, was superb. He helped in giving me a balance between over-keenness and sincerity, wild guesswork and actual fact, and lightheartedness and sentimentality.

In fact, Tony, I feel the outcome is like mixing a drink: there is ample gin with the exact amount of tonic, tempered with enough ice to make it nearly perfect.

There are enough ingredients in this book to make pleasant reading for the serious cricket lover and ample pleasantries for other mortals.

Thank you, Tony.

Introduction

by Trevor Bailey

NOBODY IS better qualified to write a book about wicket-keepers and wicket-keeping than Godfrey Evans. He has demonstrated and studied the art for more than half a century and the twinkle that was rarely far from his eye should not be allowed to disguise its shrewdness. It does not take 'Godders' long to spot talent behind the stumps.

He was always one of my favourite cricketers – the type of man you might bowl for nought during the heat of the day, but then Godfrey would be the first person to buy you a beer at close of play. He was a fierce competitor in the middle, but a generous friend to opponents and team-mates in the pavilion or bar.

I was delighted to accept Godfrey's offer to write the introduction for his book. He discusses wicket-keeping seriously – any youngster, or experienced 'keeper for that matter, would do well to take heed of his words of wisdom – and yet there is always an underlying trend of humour and fun.

Godfrey's famous 'mutton-chop' whiskers are a familiar sight on the cricket scene, in his working capacities for either Ladbrokes or Gordon's. He watches a lot of cricket, even today, travelling around the country in his portable home. He has the respect and friendship of two generations of cricketers and, when 'keepers seek counsel from Godfrey, as they often do, I'm sure in future he will say with a smile: 'Buy the book!'

Godfrey, quite apart from being the finest wicket-keeper I have seen, possessed a wonderfully vivid and enriched character. He could say and do things others would neither have contemplated nor got away with. To me he will always be the Max Miller of cricket, the original 'Cheeky Chappie'.

1

I often feel Godfrey's personality is out of place in the somewhat uniform age in which we live.

The wicket-keeper is the fulcrum of the fielding side and can transform the whole appearance of it. Godfrey realised this and revelled in it. His bubbling enthusiasm was an inspiration and did much to keep his team-mates going. At the end of a long, hot day in the field, Godfrey would still be chivvying and encouraging his bowlers and fielders alike. 'Another couple of wickets and we're through them,' he would say. The score might be 400 for three, but it did not matter to Godfrey.

After a day's play, Godfrey always enjoyed a drink and a party. Instinctively generous – this, combined with his inborn impetuosity, is why some of his commercial ventures did not succeed as he had hoped – he is usually the first to the bar. He can always be guaranteed to add life to a dull party. In the days when MCC travelled by ship for overseas tours, Godfrey was a constant source of fun on the long voyage.

His vivacious Carmen Miranda at the fancy-dress dance became almost legendary. On race night, Godfrey, colourfully attired, would set up as a somewhat unorthodox, quick-talking bookie – in direct opposition to the ship's Tote. Even his partners in bookmaking enterprises were often worried by the startling prices he offered during dinner. He was usually lucky, though. Indeed, Godfrey is a genuine punter, happy to celebrate a win, but never complaining when he loses. And, of course, he subscribes to the theory that there is all the more call for champagne after a loss than a win!

Godfrey was a breathtakingly talented wicket-keeper. He made catches and stumpings others would not have considered chances. People sometimes accused him of excessive flamboyance, but he missed very little. He had superb hands, balance and athleticism, and almost uncanny anticipation. I recall fielding at short-leg in the Test trial at Bradford in 1950 when Jim Laker took eight wickets for two runs. He bowled a ball to Don Keynon that lifted and turned and Don played it down in front of him. Godfrey anticipated so well that he caught the ball full-length one-handed and parallel to the batting crease. There was another occasion when Godfrey, as usual standing up to Alec Bedser, caught Neil Harvey off a middle-of-the-bat leg glance at Brisbane in 1950–51.

I have never seen Godfrey play better than he did in that series in Australia. I cannot remember his putting down a catch or missing a stumping. His outstanding match, though, was probably in South Africa in 1948–49 at Port Elizabeth, where, on a recently re-laid pitch, the ball shot along the ground at least twice an over. A wicket-keeper could not have had more difficult conditions, yet Godfrey conceded only one bye in the whole match, took six catches and hardly put a glove wrong.

Godfrey thrived on the big occasion, and as a result was generally better for England than for Kent. Apart from his natural talent and wonderful eye, he had enormous vitality. A lot of people can be brilliant for short periods of time, but Godfrey was just as full of life and spectacular actions after five successive sessions in grilling heat in Adelaide. Godfrey was fortunate in that he was able to take a nap and awake refreshed. On numerous occasions, I saw him come in at lunchtime, have a drink and then curl up and go to sleep, completely oblivious of the noise of the dressing-room. Another important reason for his success was his ability to dismiss instantly from his mind any mistake he might make. The next ball was the one that mattered. Very occasionally he did have a bad day, most notably at Leeds in 1948, when Australia scored more than 400 on the last day to win. Godfrey, who was certainly not alone in dropping catches, even thought that he might never again be selected for England. Altogether he played in 91 Test matches.

I played in more than 50 Tests with Godfrey and probably shared in more partnerships with him than anybody. His batting was often underestimated. He was not brilliant and often contented himself with a bright and breezy knock in county cricket. He scored a thousand runs in a season more than once, though, and in fact enjoyed his best season when somebody placed a sizeable bet that he would not reach four figures. Godfrey always rose to a challenge.

3

Many of our partnerships were rearguard actions, when our respective techniques blended well. I loved to have him at the other end. When he walked out to bat, Godfrey would strut up to me and say: 'What's been going on, Trevor? We'll knock off these runs tonight.' The fact that we might need another 250 to win with three wickets standing was immaterial.

He liked to hit hard and often and scamper enthusiastically between the wickets, often introducing a note of genuine comedy. His best innings was probably the one in which he made a century against the West Indies at Old Trafford in 1950 when, joining me at 88 for five, Godfrey scored 104 on a horrible beach of a pitch. The ball was lifting shoulder high – as well as turning – at times. We put on 161 for the sixth wicket, England recovered and we won our only Test of the rubber.

Soon after the selectors decided in 1959 to find a successor for him in the England team, Godfrey retired. He needed the added incentive of international cricket to retain his interest. He came to Kent's aid in 1967 when Alan Knott was chosen for England for the first time and, although not having kept in a county game for some years, performed superbly.

Earlier I had captained Godfrey on what he had intended to be his farewell performance. In the final match of a happy tour, the International Cavaliers were playing Barbados. But we were hit by injuries and could not even raise a fully fit side. Not wanting the match to peter out into a draw, I declared and set our opponents a target against the clock. Godfrey, despite a septic knee, insisted on keeping wicket and he put on an exhibition. He was brilliant.

Gordon's Gin
Wicket-Keepers
of the World

1

My Favourite Wicket-keepers

I WAS batting with Arthur McIntyre. We completed three runs and turned for the fourth. Seeing Bill Johnston's throw from the boundary was ten to fifteen yards off target, Arthur attempted to scamper that fourth run. It was a decision that might have lost a Test match.

Johnston's return was high and wide, but the Australian wicket-keeper leapt and, in one movement, caught the ball and threw down the wicket with his gloved hand. McIntyre was run out and England went on to lose the first Test of the 1950–51 series at Brisbane by 70 runs.

That moment will forever remain vividly etched on my memory. It provided a perfect illustration of the genius of Australia's wicket-keeper that day, Don Tallon. He is the best 'keeper I have seen. Forget Knott, Marsh or Taylor; forget Engineer, Waite or Oldfield; forget Murray, Maddocks or Langley. Magnificent wicket-keepers all of them, but Don Tallon, the unobtrusive artist from Queensland, stands supreme.

Tallon, his safe hands allied to lightning reflexes, could make the most improbable dismissals look outrageously straightforward. He played much of his cricket on the placid pitches at Brisbane, where the ball would rarely deviate, and, as a result, needed to work hard for many of his victims. Chances were a rarity and many 'keepers playing at the 'Gabba' came to regret a momentary lapse in concentration in the morning session, as the very batsman they had allowed to 'escape' piled on the runs late into the afternoon.

Perhaps to compensate for the fact that the odds were loaded in the batsman's favour at Brisbane, Tallon gained a

reputation for gamesmanship. It used to be said that he
would get you out by 'fair means or foul'. But nobody
disputed his brilliance.

Decades later, I am still mystified about why he was
omitted from the Australian team that toured England in
1938. Ben Barnett was chosen instead, but Tallon showed
the qualities the Australian selectors had overlooked by
breaking two world records the following winter.

Against New South Wales in 1938–39, Tallon shared in
twelve dismissals (six in each innings – nine caught and
three stumped). Only Edward Pooley, for Surrey against
Sussex at The Oval in 1868, and Brian Taber, New South
Wales v. South Australia at Adelaide in 1968–69, have
equalled the feat. A few weeks later, Tallon joined only a
handful of other wicket-keepers by disposing of seven
Victoria batsmen (three caught, four stumped) at Brisbane.
Wally Grout has subsequently secured the first-class record
outright by catching eight Western Australian batsmen,
playing for Queensland at Brisbane in 1959–60.

Tallon would assuredly have toured England in 1942 but
for the intervention of the War. When Bradman brought his
triumphant side over in 1948, Tallon was the automatic
choice.

Although quite tall for a wicket-keeper, around 5 ft
10½ in, Tallon was exceptionally fleet of foot. He moved to
take the ball late, not committing himself until he had
watched for any movement off the pitch, and would remain
largely unnoticed – a sure sign of a high-class wicket-
keeper. Then, quite suddenly when spotting a chance, he
would fling himself to take a catch or remove the bails in an
instant.

The first time I played against Don in a Test match was at
Sydney in 1946–47, the game in which Syd Barnes and Don
Bradman each scored 234 and England lost by an innings
and 33 runs. In the first innings, Tallon caught Denis
Compton from a rebound off the slip fielder's chest. Colin
McCool was bowling at the time and the catch showed
Tallon's eye for a dismissal, even in the most unlikely
circumstances. The possibility of a catch would not have
entered most wicket-keepers' minds.

Bertie Oldfield, Tallon's predecessor, passed on a great deal of advice to him. Oldfield was a magnificent stylist. Few stumpers can have kept to greater bowlers than the speed men Macdonald and Gregory, and to Grimmett and O'Reilly. Those two great spin bowlers' ability to lure batsmen out of their ground was principally responsible for Oldfield's high percentage of stumpings – 52 out of 130 dismissals in Test cricket.

That same Bill O'Reilly, in one of his articles towards the end of that 1946–47 tour – he later became a hard-hitting writer – declared: 'There is only one department in which England could claim to equal Australia. That is Godfrey Evans' performance behind the stumps. He has shown that he can keep wicket equally as well as our own great Don Tallon.' I could have been paid no greater compliment.

Tallon dismissed twenty batsmen against Wally Hammond's team that winter. The proliferation of Test matches in recent years has allowed that figure to be bettered quite frequently; but at the time only Herbert Strudwick, with twenty-one for England against South Africa in 1913–14, had enjoyed a more prolific rubber.

Immediately after the War, Tallon was probably at the height of his powers. He was equally adept standing back or standing up, which he frequently did to bowlers of medium-pace and above, and his gathering of returns was magnificent. His excellence inspired both bowlers and fieldsmen; and I know many England batsmen felt a sense of impending woe when Don was behind the stumps. He was not a bad batsman, either, scoring more than 6,000 runs at almost 30. It seems staggering that Don Tallon played in only twenty-one Test matches because, in my view, he was the most complete wicket-keeper of all time.

England, though, have also had a fair share of men with golden gloves. Alan Knott and Bob Taylor, our two outstanding 'keepers of the modern era, are dealt with in another chapter, together with Rodney Marsh of Australia.

Les Ames, part of the Kent tradition of 'keepers, was also a great batsman, who scored 102 first-class centuries. One of my regrets is that I never saw Les at his peak because, when I took over from him for Kent just before the War, he had been suffering with an injured back. Another fine Kent wicket-keeper, and a man who taught me a lot, was Howard ('Hopper') Levett. He had the misfortune of his career running parallel to that of Ames, but Hopper, a wonderfully engaging personality but prone to inconsistency, was the best in the country on his day.

There was one occasion when Hopper, still feeling the effects of a long and heavy night, remained completely motionless as the first ball of the following morning sped past him and disappeared over the boundary for four byes. Next delivery, the batsman got an edge and Hopper plunged far to his left and held a miraculous catch. He got up and announced triumphantly: 'Not bad for the first ball of the morning!'

One of my favourite wicket-keepers was John Murray. It was impossible for 'JT' to be inelegant. His style bordered on perfection and, before each delivery, he would touch his cap and his gloves together before settling down. JT was always immaculately turned out, such a delight on a cricket field, and even the way he passed the ball to the slips was graceful. While playing for Middlesex in 1975, he established a world record, taking it from Herbert Strudwick, by reaching 1,527 first-class dismissals – 1,270 catches and 257 stumpings. Bob Taylor surpassed Murray's figure in 1983.

JT was also a fine batsman, good enough to score a superb 112 against the West Indies at The Oval in 1966, a match in which England recovered from 166 for seven to reach 527 all out. John was the man regarded as most likely to follow me in the England team, but injury in India in 1961–62 and again in Australia in 1962–63 deprived him of a regular Test place and restricted his international appearances to twenty-one, coincidentally the same number as Tallon had had.

But, if John Murray's Test career was limited, it is even more amazing to think that Keith Andrew played only twice for England. His county career began in 1952 and extended until 1966, and for a number of years he was considered by most players as the best wicket-keeper in England. Neat, skilful and unobtrusive, Andrew took part in 903 dismissals in his career. He captained Northamptonshire from 1962 to 1966, during which time they finished eighth, seventh, third, second and fifth in the County Championship – a period of sustained success for a county who have never won the ultimate domestic prize. Keith is now passing on his knowledge as Director of Coaching to the National Cricket Association.

Jim Parks was particularly effective when standing back to the quicker bowlers and this is reflected in the fact that an unusually low proportion of his dismissals were stumped – 93 out of 1,182. Despite a pronounced square-on stance, Parks was a fine batsman who represented England for his batting only. He played as a batsman against Pakistan in 1954 and was picked as first-choice wicket-keeper a decade later. Two of his 51 first-class centuries were in Test cricket, perhaps most notably when he was summoned to bolster England's batting in the West Indies in 1959–60. He scored 43 and 101 not out in the fifth Test in Port-of-Spain and 183 in his only other innings on the tour.

Dick Spooner of Warwickshire, who was my deputy on the West Indies tour in 1953–54 under Len Hutton's captaincy, was another fine 'keeper from the same era. Leslie Compton's ability behind Middlesex stumps was enhanced by his footballing commitments with Arsenal. He had speed and fitness and, being a big man, Leslie had a telescopic reach and was never afraid to dive about.

Arnold Long of Surrey, and latterly captain of Sussex, was a dependable 'keeper, as was Jimmy Binks. He played in a remarkable 412 consecutive first-class matches for Yorkshire, testimony to his constitution as much as anything else. Binks played from 1955 to 1975 and finished with 1,071 dismissals and two England caps. It is no exaggeration to describe him as the Bob Taylor of his day.

The incomparable Tallon has not been Australia's only top-class 'keeper. Indeed, not everybody shared my opinion that Tallon was the best. Keith Miller once told me that he thought Gil Langley was the safest and finest wicket-keeper in Australia from the start of his (Langley's) career in 1945 to its conclusion in 1957.

Langley possessed neither Oldfield's polish nor Tallon's speed of glove, yet he possibly made fewer errors than either. Langley certainly did not look the archetypal sporting hero. A powerful, thick-set, almost overweight man, he squatted behind the stumps with his right foot flat and left heel raised, waiting for the bowler to arrive. Unusually, his gloves were held together in front of his knees, rather than touching the ground. But, my word, he was consistent. Gil broke my own record of Test dismissals in a series in England with 19 against us in 1956 – and in just three Test matches in which he played. (I took 16 against Australia in 1953; both figures have since been exceeded.)

Len Maddocks and Ron Saggers, two other Australians, were unfortunate to remain largely in the shadows of Langley and Don Tallon. Maddocks was not flashy nor showy, but extremely competent and he played in seven Test matches. He is now an influential member of the Australian Cricket Board who, as manager of the ill-fated 1977 Australian touring team to England, discovered that most of his players had already signed for Packer. He handled an awkward situation with admirable diplomacy in an effort to maintain a united front.

Saggers did not let Australia down in his six Tests; his style was neat, and in some ways he was reminiscent of Oldfield. In the early part of his career, Saggers was considered a good enough batsman to be selected for New South Wales for his batting alone.

Clyde Walcott was one of the West Indies' finest all-round cricketers: a useful bowler and batsman who could hit murderously hard. He was selected as a wicket-keeper batsman in the early part of his career and, having a similar build to Leslie Compton, took some fabulous catches by using his enormous reach.

Farokh Engineer is probably the finest wicket-keeper to have come out of India. A smile was never far from his face and he made sure he was constantly at the centre of things when India were in the field. His athleticism allowed Engineer to reach the widest leg glances and few 'keepers have ever removed the bails more rapidly. A total of 82 of his 824 first-class dismissals were in Test cricket. A marvellous, instinctive batsman, Farokh was a joy to watch, and he opened the batting for his country. His extrovert person-

12

ality made him popular with the Lancashire crowds and he was a significant figure in that county's success in one-day cricket in the late sixties and early seventies.

Johnny Waite, the only cricketer to appear in fifty or more Tests for South Africa, was a tall man and what I would describe as a quiet perfectionist behind the stumps. His handling of spin bowling was very clean and Waite was also capable of taking spectacular catches standing back. He was selected for South Africa's tour of England in 1951 as reserve wicket-keeper, but, after performing well in the opening matches, was picked for the first Test and never looked back. While Australia amassed 520 in the fifth Test at Melbourne in 1952–53, Waite did not concede a single bye. As a batsman, Waite's defence was sound and, despite a short backlift, had a full range of strokes. He scored four Test centuries and made 2,405 runs at more than 30.

2

Bowlers I Have Kept To

WICKET-KEEPERS NEED good bowlers. The majority of dismissals are completed by the 'keeper merely delivering the *coup de grâce* after the bowler has lured the batsman into an error. High-quality bowling will keep 'keepers happy; but they will curse if bowlers are spraying the ball 'all over the shop'.

One of my darkest early cricketing memories is of playing in a club match in the Weald of Kent in my first year on the county staff. The pitch was rough and long grass covered the outfield. My team were under the illusion that they were the best in Kent and each bowler in turn attempted impersonations of Harold Larwood, with scant regard for line or length. Every bowler charged in and slung the ball as hard as he could. As a result, it would arrive to me either on the third bounce or so wide that I needed to dive full-length to get even close to it. Not only was it irritating and hard work, maintaining concentration was virtually impossible; when the ball legitimately beat the bat or a chance was given, I simply was not ready for it.

After that nightmare match, I appreciated our own staff bowlers like *Wally Carter, Harry Bowers* and *Colin Cole* even more when I returned to Canterbury. Dejected, I reported my failure to Ted Humphries, our head coach and an understanding man. Ted's sympathetic response was: 'It is all part of your education, Godfrey. Don't let it worry you. Those village lads will soon notice the difference when you are not there next week. You just concentrate on the next game.'

I was fortunate to have a thorough grounding keeping wicket to all types of bowling in my early years at Kent. For example, when I joined the county as a young colt, I had no experience of standing back. I thought a 'keeper should stand up, no matter how fast the bowler was. I remember standing up to *Jack Martin* in a Minor Counties match against Middlesex at Sittingbourne, primarily to preserve my ego, and immediately dropping three catches. Jack was livid, and rightly so, because he had asked me to stand back.

To emphasise my folly, I was keeping when Jack opened the bowling on his debut for England against South Africa at Trent Bridge in 1947. 'Bustler' Martin, as we called him – he used to bustle back to his mark (I wish all bowlers did that nowadays) – delivered his first ball in Test cricket. It began harmlessly enough outside the off stump but, after it had passed the wicket, suddenly veered down the legside. I had learned my lesson by now and was standing back, but the ball still eluded my dive and went for four byes!

Norman Harding was another fast bowler on the staff. He possessed an excellent away-swinger and the number of snicks he induced made me realise that catching the ball was much easier when able to follow its course standing back. Norman was tall, had an excellent run-up, and with his double loop arm action he created a fine position for delivery. He was an outstanding candidate for a prosperous career; his death in 1947, at the age of 31, was a sad blow to Kent cricket.

I also gained experience of pace by keeping to Wally Carter, who probably helped me more than any other bowler in those early days, even though he always asked me to stand up. I also went up to the stumps for *Alan Watt*, medium-pace, and *Leslie Todd*, a left-arm medium-pacer and also a fine batsman. They were ideal to stand up to and I completed several legside stumpings off both of them – a feature that has virtually disappeared from the game.

The Kent spinners also provided plenty of variety. *Doug Wright*, quick leg-spin, was the best in the business on his day and, like his predecessor 'Tich' Freeman, had a flair for the game – although in a different way. Whereas Tich was particularly adept at running through the lower order,

Doug could eliminate the first five in any batting team. His speed, allied to his ability to turn the ball prodigiously, troubled even the best batsmen on plumb pitches. Other slow bowlers who played for the county and were always willing to give me practice included *Ray Dovey, Claude Lewis*, who later became the county's scorer, and *Fred Foy*. So I quickly gained experience at keeping to all types of bowling – fast, slow, standing up, standing back. It stood me in good stead for the rest of my career.

With the outbreak of War, professional cricket was suspended, but after I joined the Army I was given the opportunity to further my education. I played with – and kept to – bowlers such as *'Gubby' Allen, Tony Mallett, Trevor Bailey*, then a young Marine, and even *Maurice Tate*. Maurice's action and ability to make the ball gather pace off the pitch was amazing. I remember clearly a match in which, probably, I first established something of a reputation. I managed three legside stumpings off a Surrey pro called *Freddie Pierpoint*, bowling at a lively pace, against Arthur Gilligan's RAF side at the Officers' Ground at Aldershot. I also recall keeping in a match at Lord's while Learie Constantine was batting. I found it extraordinary that, although his feet were all over the place, he still managed to hit the ball hard. He had such a magnificent eye.

I was unable to play in the Victory Tests against Australia because I was posted to Germany and my CO, not a keen cricket fan, hardly bent over backwards to help my cause. So my career resumed properly in 1946, when Kent had another young fast bowler on the staff in *Fred Ridgway*. He was small of stature, but well-proportioned, with a rather strained and ugly run-up; but he was in an excellent side-on position at the moment of delivery. Fred was not so much a swing bowler, relying more on hitting the deck with the ball and extracting movement off the pitch. He could, though, sometimes make it wobble, float, dip and, because of his size, keep low. This often made taking his bowling an awkward business, but it ensured that I watched the ball right into my gloves. In many ways Fred Ridgway was unlucky, because he was in his prime at a time when England had a proliferation of good fast-medium bowlers.

Consequently, he was limited to five Test appearances and toured with MCC only once – to India in 1951–52. He took four wickets in consecutive balls against Derbyshire at Folkestone in 1951.

Among the other seam bowlers with Kent after the War were *Eddie Crush* (I once caught Don Bradman off his bowling and did not appeal!), *Alan Shirreff*, from the RAF and one-time captain of the Combined Services, and ex-Warwickshire and New Zealand fast bowler *Tom Pritchard*, whom I considered to be the fastest bowler in England for a time.

Doug Wright remained our premier spinner. He was assisted by Ray Dovey (off-spin) and Claude Lewis (left-arm) as well as *Jack Pettiford*, a leg-spinner and batsman from Australia. I clearly remember the time he dismissed Peter May for 99 with a full toss at Blackheath.

I kept wicket to all these men while playing for Kent, but, of course, there were dozens of other county bowlers of whom I got a batsman's eye view. I also kept to a wide selection when playing for England, on tours and in games such as Gentlemen v. Players. And, of all of them, my partnership with *Alec Bedser* was probably the most famous. Alec had no peer as a fast-medium bowler. I always maintain that he developed his astonishing accuracy on the 1946–47 tour to Australia, when he was forced to do a tremendous amount of work on good pitches. This made him learn to bowl to a field and, having mastered that, he started to vary his pace and develop his leg-cutter. I remember Alec bowling Lindsay Hassett in the Brisbane Test of the 1950–51 series. Lindsay went to play the delivery towards mid-wicket but, to his amazement, the ball cut across him and hit his off stump. I was as relieved as anyone – I had committed myself to the legside and if the ball had not hit the stumps, it would have gone for four byes.

Alec's leg-cutter would go like a quick leg-break, even on a pitch that might resemble a pudding. One time, in our early days, I was standing back to him on a damp pitch. Alec beat the bat with a real beauty but watched despairingly as the ball dropped gently into my gloves. He mumbled: 'This wicket is much too slow for me.' Before the next

18

delivery, I dashed up to the stumps. Alec again man-oeuvred the ball past the outside edge of the bat. This time, though, I was standing up and whipped off the bails and shouted like mad for a stumping. In truth, I knew the batsman had not lifted his foot, but it revived Alec instan-taneously. 'Give me that ball, Godders,' he said, 'this is just the pitch I've been waiting for.' Just another example of how the stumper can help the bowlers and fielders.

There was another occasion when Alec was bowling to Arthur Morris, the Australian left-hander. He moved away from Arthur, but the thin edge flew past Denis Compton, who was standing very wide at slip.

'Where do you want me, Alec?' asked Denis, gesticulat-ing with his arms.

'You'd better come where you should have been in the first place – a bit finer,' came Alec's agitated reply.

Denis moved a pace or two to his right and, from the very next ball, Arthur got a thick edge and the ball sped past the exact spot where Denis had been positioned and to the boundary for four. You should have heard Alec cursing his luck.

'Now where do you want me, Alec?' said Denis with a twinkle in his eye.

'Where do I want you? I want another bloody fielder.'

Denis and I were chuckling for the remainder of the over. Then we went over and said: 'Well bowled, Alec.' Even Alec saw the funny side of it. He was a magnificent bowler.

Even at the age of 45, *'Gubby' Allen* still had a marvellous action, a smooth run-up culminating in a high leap and quick shoulder and arm action. This meant that he released the ball from a considerable height, compensating for his relative lack of inches for a fast bowler. He said to me at one point during the 1947–48 series in the Caribbean: 'Godfrey, I'm going to bowl a bouncer to Frank Worrell.' It was important that he warned me – I was standing up – and this short-pitched one discomfited Worrell. Next ball he was out and I could see Gubby glowing with pride.

Bill Voce, who, along with Harold Larwood, Bill Bowes and Allen, created such havoc on the 'bodyline' tour, was another bowler who played most of his cricket before the

War. His left-arm, over the wicket bowling was still distinctly sharp after the War and, with his high action, often made the ball lift up towards the right-hander's rib-cage. During the 1946–47 tour of Australia, I was keeping to Bill in an up-country match. The batsman played forward, missed the ball and over-balanced. I was standing back – what else to Bill? – and, seeing the batsman out of his ground, gathered the ball and aimed at the wicket. Luck was on my side as the ball hit the stumps. 'You must be getting slow in your old age, Bill,' I joked. 'Stumped Evans, bowled Voce. They will never believe that in England.'

Bill Copson, too, lost many good years to the War. He generated lift from his type of slinging action and, in many ways, was a right-handed Bill Voce. He bowled above medium-pace and, although his arm was not high, he could make the ball break back alarmingly. His first wicket in county cricket was that of Andy Sandham at The Oval in 1932 and his 140 wickets in 1936 contributed much to Derbyshire's first Championship win. He toured Australia in 1936–37 and, although topping the averages, he did not appear in a Test match. His first Test appearance was against the West Indies at Lord's in 1939. Copson took nine wickets and England won easily.

Nottinghamshire produced a number of outstanding fast bowlers either side of the War. Harold Larwood and Voce, of course, and *Harold Butler*, who did not come to prominence until Larwood retired. Butler's approach to the stumps was ungainly but, at the point of delivery, everything was right. If Butler had a fault, it was that he bowled too short, affording the great players that extra split second in which to play their shots. Pitching up an extra foot or two would have gained him plenty more wickets, although Harold did take almost 1,000 in his first-class career. He once took eight for 15 against Surrey at Trent Bridge, six clean bowled.

Ken Cranston's nagging accuracy brought rewards, like the time he took four wickets in an over against South Africa at Headingley in 1947. He enjoyed life, and his career was shortened by his desire to concentrate on his dental practice. Ken, well-built and tireless, was also a capable batsman and captained Lancashire for two seasons. *Dick Pollard*, another Lancastrian, was a mover off the pitch rather than a swinger in the air. He seemed to get better the more he bowled and was never anything other than accurate. He knocked back Don Bradman's stumps with an absolute beauty in the first innings at Leeds in 1948. It was a pity he could not do it again in the second innings – Don scored 173 not out and Australia made 404 for three on the last day to win. I have always regretted dropping Bradman twice off Dick's bowling in the state match against South Australia in Adelaide in 1946–47. I am sure those errors kept Dick out of the Tests in that series.

Keeping to *Norman Yardley* was always great fun. Norman's medium-pacers appeared so innocuous, but he had so many good players in trouble. His natural arm action made the ball wobble and he had the knack of deviating it off the seam as well. He held a high number of return catches – often from his well-disguised slower ball – and although he took only 21 Test wickets, he accounted for Bradman three times. *Freddie Brown*, normally a leg-spinner, turned to bowling seam up, in similar style to Normans, when he captained our side in Australia in 1950–51, and he achieved considerable success.

Derek Shackleton of Hampshire was possibly the unluckiest bowler of his generation. He made only seven Test appearances – the first of them against West Indies on a shirtfront at Trent Bridge in 1950. Frank Worrell scored 261 and Everton Weekes 129; the West Indies amassed 558, and 'Shack's' first innings figures were one for 128. Perhaps he was not quite pacey enough for a really good Test wicket, but he produced some wonderful performances in county cricket. He stands seventh on the all-time list with 2,857 first-class wickets. Only Wilf Rhodes (23) has taken 100 wickets in a season more than Shack's 20 times. He joined Hampshire as a batsman who bowled bad leg-breaks, but the county, who were short of seam bowlers, tried him in that style and he was a revelation. His action was light, easy and wristy and he moved the ball both ways off the seam. Perhaps Derek's most stunning quality was his accuracy. Desmond Eagar, Hampshire's captain at the time, said of

21

Shack in 1964 – he was then in his 40th year – 'I actually saw him bowl a long-hop.' That just about summed it up. Shack bowled one long-hop and two half-volleys a season. He made a telling contribution to Hampshire's County Championship victory in 1961, under Colin Ingleby-Mackenzie's captaincy.

Derbyshire's *Les Jackson*, whose two Test appearances were separated by twelve years, was another bowler who never gave up. He had a slinging action, bringing the ball from behind his back, and could nip it back off the seam or lift it quite sharply. His new-ball partnership for Derbyshire with *Cliff Gladwin* was one of the best in the country. Gladwin dismissed many batsmen by having them caught at leg slip from one of his booming inswingers. Gladwin, going down the pavilion steps at the end of the exciting Durban Test of 1948–49, muttered the immortal comment: 'Cometh the hour, cometh the man.' England won by two wickets with a leg bye off the final ball of the match.

Peter Loader's greatest asset was his change of pace – he could bowl a genuinely fast bouncer and a well-disguised slower ball. There was a hint of a throw or jerk in his wristy action and he was no-balled on one or two occasions for chucking, but he was much quicker than he looked. He bowled superbly in the first innings of the first Test at Brisbane against Australia in 1958–59, taking four for 56. In the second innings, with Australia wanting 147 to win, Loader's opening spell was full of hostility. I could feel he was losing his edge, though, when the ball stopped smacking into my gloves with the same force as at the start of his spell.

I said to Peter May, our captain: 'I think Peter has just about had it.'

But the skipper did not take the hint. So I again mentioned that, perhaps, it would be better to give Loader a rest, otherwise he would be too tired to return to have a shot at the tail-enders. May thanked me, but left poor old Peter on.

Even Trevor Bailey came up to me and said: 'Don't you think you should tell the captain to give Peter a rest?' 'I did that two overs ago,' was my reply. Australia eventually won by eight wickets with Norman O'Neill, in his first Test, scoring 71 not out.

It was off Peter Loader that I equalled Bertie Oldfield's record of 130 Test dismissals with a diving catch from an inside edge by Fazal Mahmood against Pakistan at The Oval in 1954.

Trevor Bailey, a fine all-rounder and intelligent cricketer, was a magnificent servant to England. His greatest bowling performance was against the West Indies at Sabina Park, Kingston, in 1953–54. Trevor took seven for 34 and moved the ball more on a perfect wicket than anybody I have seen. England's win in that fifth Test enabled us to draw the series.

Trevor was also a Test-class batsman, famed for his stubborn rearguard actions. He was batting with his usual solidity at The Oval in 1953 – the match in which we clinched the Ashes – and I was at the other end going quite fluently for a change. I turned the ball towards fine leg and called for a run (thinking of two). Trevor shouted 'No.' But I had dashed off, turned, slipped and failed to make my ground and was run out by Alan Davidson for 28. Afterwards, I was speaking to Alan about the incident and he told me he had forgotten to go deep, because he was talking to the umpire. He should have been on the boundary.

And then, of course, we come to *Fred Trueman, Brian Statham* and *Frank Tyson*. Fred had a marvellous run-up and perfect side-on action, allowing him to bowl the outswinger so well. You never knew what Fred would send down next – a swinging full-toss, a fast yorker, a bouncer. Fred believed that he never bowled a ball that did not move or swing. He never gave up, though, and would come back for the last two or three overs of the day with just the same enthusiasm as at the start.

Statham was the straightest of the three, always on the spot, and was different from Fred in that he relied more on movement off the pitch than on swing. I caught Jackie McGlew off Brian from the first ball of South Africa's first innings in the Lord's Test in 1955. In the second innings of that match, 'George' Statham captured seven for 39.

Tyson was the quickest bowler in the world during the

1954–55 series in Australia. Although his run-up was un-gainly, he generated enormous pace from his broad shoulders and long, sinewy arms – a physical characteristic common to many fast bowlers (their arm somehow cuts through the air better).

Men such as Trueman had superb actions, but *Don Bennett*, the former Middlesex opening bowler, might even have had too perfect an action. The first time I saw him, I noted his action and thought he would almost certainly play for England. When this did not happen, I wanted to know why. I came to the conclusion that Don, with his easy run and fluent delivery stride, allowed the batsman a good view of the ball even before it left his hand, thus eliminating the element of surprise.

These, then, are the fast and medium-pace bowlers who remain most vividly etched on my memory. What about the spinners, a brand of bowler that presents a totally different set of problems to a wicket-keeper?

Early in my cricketing life, the leg-spinner was prominent, but by the time I retired, off-spinners were coming more to the fore. Wicket-keepers miss more chances off spin bowling than any other type, especially when the pitch is turning. A spinner is always looking to make the batsman drive and, for this to happen, the ball must be well pitched up, almost to half-volley length. So when the bat comes into position to drive, it obscures the ball for a crucial split-second. So, if the ball turns, and usually it must to beat the bat, the 'keeper often does not have sufficient time to move into the correct position and focus on the ball. As a result, apparently straightforward stumpings or catches missed by a 'keeper standing up to spin bowling are more difficult than they look.

I dropped Bradman in this way off *Jim Laker*, the finest off-spinner I have seen. Jim could make the ball dip and still keep it well pitched up. I recall how he lured Jimmy Burke out of his ground in the Lord's Test of 1956 and I completed the legside stumping. Jim once said to me: 'Godfrey, I once played with a club 'keeper, who stood about a yard-and-a-half away from the wicket to take my bowling. And he often made a stumping by catching the ball and running to the

Standing around 5ft 2ins, Tich Freeman had an extraordinary wicket-taking record for Kent between the wars. I somehow suspect this photograph was posed – I don't recall Tich leaping over a fence and avoiding a couple of trees in the middle of his run-up! *South Eastern Newspapers*

Ray Lindwall in full flight. The great Australian fast bowler at the point of delivery during the fifth Test match at The Oval in 1953. *The Photo Source*

wicket and removing the bails before the batsman got back.' It might have suited this particular club 'keeper, but I must say I cannot see many first-class stumpers adopting the method! It showed, though, Jim's capacity for getting batsmen stranded a long way down the pitch. Jim had a reputation for not bowling so well when the batsmen were getting after him, but in my opinion it was quite undeserved.

Of the other off-spinners, *Roy Tattersall* had a longer run than most and was more of a cutter than a spinner who varied his pace well. *Brian Close* could turn the ball a great distance, but was erratic. Perhaps he should have concentrated on either his spinners or medium-pacers, with which he sometimes took the new ball. *Alan Oakman*, a tall man, could extract bounce, and I always remember stumping the one and only Peter May off Alan's bowling at Lord's. I was his friend for life after that. *Bob Appleyard*, primarily a cutter of the ball, could be devastating when the pitch was giving assistance. He took 200 wickets at 14.14 in 1951, his first full season, but his career was dogged by ill health. Appleyard was a sort of right-handed Derek Underwood.

Doug Wright was, for me, the finest leg-spinner of the last 50 years. Although his control was suspect at times, Doug combined speed and spin, so that keeping wicket to him was very exciting. He came bounding in off a long run for a spinner, and I was always on the lookout for the signal he gave for his quicker ball. I suppose Doug was something of an enigma. At his destructive best, he was almost unplayable – he took a world record seven hat-tricks – and sometimes he would make the ball turn and lift so sharply that it evaded the 'keeper's reach. He played in 34 Tests, but his 108 wickets cost 39.11 each – the highest average for any bowler with more than 100 victims in Test cricket. He took more than 2,000 wickets and Bradman, among others, held him in high regard. Doug later became a much-loved coach at Charterhouse.

John Ikin spun the ball more than *Eric Hollies* and delivered it in more of a loop. Eric, on the other hand, tended to roll it out the back of his hand and, therefore, was more accurate. Hollies's greatest moment was, of course, when he bowled Bradman with a googly second ball at The Oval in 1948. The Don, in his last innings in Test cricket, had been given three cheers by the England team and applauded all the way to the wicket. Was there a tear in his eye, I wonder?

Jim Sims of Middlesex – the spinner – and Essex's *Peter Smith* – the roller – were a similarly contrasting pair. Peter took nine wickets in an innings against New South Wales in Australia in 1946–47. I was keeping wicket that day and, to be honest, most of his victims were caught on the boundary, so it was not such a good performance as it looked. It did get him into the team for the final Test, but he did not bowl well.

'Roley' Jenkins gave the ball so much air that you felt there was a chance of a stumping from every ball. I can understand why Hugo Yarnold, the Worcestershire 'keeper, captured so many victims off the bowling of Roley, Peter Jackson and Dick Howorth.

Both *Ken Barrington* and *Tom Graveney*, both brilliant batsmen, were also useful, and decidedly keen, leg-break bowlers. I think they should have been used more. *Tommy Greenhough*, the Lancashire 'leggie', gave me more trouble than anybody and, in fact, it was a poor performance keeping to his bowling that finished my Test career. In the second Test against India at Lord's in 1959, I missed four stumpings in two overs from Tommy and that, coupled with being bowled for nought after I was struck on the temple by a ball from their opening bowler, Desai, signalled the end. I was never picked for England again.

Of the left-arm spinners, I enjoyed keeping to *Johnny Wardle*. He could change his action so much that, even on good wickets, I always felt there was a chance of a victim. And his variations of flight were expert. Johnny was a fine bowler and great entertainer, often trying to kid the batsman into taking an extra run by pretending he had missed the ball in the field. Then, just as the batsman was about to run, Johnny would fling the ball in. *Jack Young* of Middlesex was quite a character, too. He bowled eleven consecutive maidens to Sid Barnes and Bradman at Trent Bridge in 1948 – which was no mean feat – and his final figures were

60–28–79–1. While in South Africa, a ball from Jack knocked out three of my front teeth when it pitched in the blockhole, came straight up and hit me in the mouth.

Neither *Bob Berry* nor *Malcolm Hilton* realised his early potential, although Hilton, when just 19, dismissed Bradman twice in Lancashire's match against the Australians in 1948.

Jack Walsh of Leicestershire bowled left-arm googlies and 'chinamen' and spun the ball more than any of the left-armers, and I recall stumping Donald Carr – who did not spot the googly – off his bowling during a Gentlemen v. Players match at Lord's. Worcestershire's *Dick Howorth* was quicker than most. Dick had Dyer of South Africa caught at cover with his first ball in Test cricket and was so surprised he simply burst out laughing.

Denis Compton was no mug with the ball, either. He started as an orthodox left-arm spinner, but switched to chinamen and googlies. His early overs before lunch on the final day against Australia at Headingley in 1948 were the best I saw him bowl. He caught and bowled Lindsay Hassett, I missed a chance to stump Arthur Morris, and Jack Crapp twice dropped Bradman at slip off Denis. I am told there was total panic in the Australian dressing-room, with the next four batsmen all trying to pad up at the same time. But those missed chances were crucial, and centuries by Morris and Bradman saw Australia to a famous seven-wicket victory.

One left-armer whom I will always remember is *James Langridge* of Sussex, simply because he was the first bowler from whom I conceded a bye in Test cricket. It was on my debut against India at The Oval in 1946 and such a silly mistake, too. I took it for granted that the ball would come into my gloves and took my eye off it. The ball kept low and went for the only bye of the innings.

3

Les Ames – My Cricketing Hero

EVERY MAN who becomes a professional sportsman must, as a wide-eyed youngster, have an inspiration. Something or someone that makes him decide he wants to earn a living from playing sport. There are bound to be ten-year-olds all over the country who have watched Ian Botham smash a six and decided: 'That is for me.' Of course, only a minute percentage actually fulfil their dreams.

My inspiration was four words: 'Stumped Ames, bowled Freeman.' I recall buying the morning paper just to read those magic words. I would be so disappointed if it had not happened the previous day. But it usually had. Reading those words prompted me to become a wicket-keeper. Les Ames was my idol and I followed his career from my schooldays.

At school, it was customary for the master to put a fat boy behind the stumps – I suppose working on the theory that he presented the biggest barricade and was, therefore, most likely to stop the ball. Being reasonably fit and athletic, I was required to bat and bowl. One day the fat boy was away, so I asked if I could have a go at wicket-keeping. I wanted to pretend to be Les Ames. I dropped the first couple of balls, but then started to get the hang of it. Ever since, I have never been anything other than a wicket-keeper.

I believe Les Ames is the greatest wicket-keeper/batsman who has ever drawn breath. In a career spanning 26 seasons, and interrupted by the Second World War, Ames helped in the dismissal of 1,113 batsmen, including an all-time record of 415 stumpings – mainly, of course, off the bowling of Tich Freeman. He scored more than 37,000

29

runs and hit 102 centuries – both unapproached figures for a wicket-keeper. Eight of his centuries came in Test cricket.

Off the field, he has also made an enormous contribution. He was a Test selector and, during his time as secretary of Kent, the county's previously ebbing finances and playing fortunes improved. Playing and administrative colleagues alike responded to his infectious personality and sheer talent.

Les would have got into almost any side for his batting alone. They did not call him 'Twinkletoes' for nothing. He hated being tied down. If he thought the bowlers were getting on top, he would do his best to reverse the situation – perhaps by dancing down the pitch to the spinners. Sometimes this positive approach brought about his downfall, but on many other occasions it prompted a dazzling display.

One of the busiest days I had during my time on the Kent groundstaff was at Dover in 1937. Gloucestershire were all out on the final afternoon leaving Kent a target of 218 runs to win in under two hours. Scoring at more than nine runs an over, Kent knocked them off in just 71 minutes. I was working the scoreboard, struggling to change the numbers quickly enough, and I don't think I've perspired so much in my life!

Bill Ashdown and Frank Woolley went in first and Les Ames went out to bat when Frank was dismissed for 44. Les scored 70 in 36 minutes, hammering the ball all over the place. Alan Watt made 39 in just 10 minutes. Ashdown was left not out with 62 in 71 minutes – and amazingly the crowd were barracking him because his rate of progress seemed so pedestrian in comparison with the others. Remember, the Gloucestershire attack that day included the great off-spinner Tom Goddard (82–0–98–0) and Reg Sinfield (9–0–69–2), the left-armer.

Of course, Les had his disappointments. He went to Australia in 1928–29 as the second wicket-keeper, but primarily as a batsman. George Duckworth, first choice behind the stumps, played in the first Test at Brisbane. England won by 675 runs and kept virtually the same side throughout the series, and Les did not play in a Test. That match at Brisbane, incidentally, was Don Bradman's first Test. Did the manner of Australia's defeat – England refused to enforce the follow-on and ultimately won by the largest run margin in Test history – help forge Don's future outlook? He certainly never relaxed his resolve to destroy all bowling, even after he had completed his first, second or third century. He was dropped after the first Test for the only time in his international career.

England's batting line-up that winter in Australia was formidable. It included Jack Hobbs, Patsy Hendren, Wally Hammond, Ernest Tyldesley, Philip Mead, Herbert Sutcliffe and Ames, each of whom ultimately scored a hundred hundreds. They had a combined career total of 1,040 centuries. Add to them Maurice Leyland, with 80 centuries, and Douglas Jardine, with 35, and it is clear why that England touring team is considered probably the strongest batting side to leave these shores. Mead and Tyldesley played only one Test each in that rubber and Ames none.

Les eventually made his Test debut against South Africa in 1929 after 'Duckie' had a couple of bad matches. With, among others, Hobbs and Sutcliffe coming towards the end of their careers, Ames soon became an automatic choice. England appreciated the value of a wicket-keeper who could be relied upon to score runs. Les kept wicket throughout the 1932–33 'bodyline' series under the captaincy of Douglas Jardine, a strict disciplinarian. There was one occasion when Les hurled himself down the legside in an effort to make a catch when the batsman got a tickle to one of Larwood's thunderbolts. Les just got his fingertips to the ball, but failed to hold it. Gubby Allen, fielding at short leg, said: 'Bad luck, Les. That was a magnificent effort.'

'Magnificent effort? He should have caught the thing in his bloody mouth,' bellowed Jardine.

Les was more or less England's first-choice until just before the Second World War, by which time he had started to suffer from back trouble. Fortunately, a bad back was something I never suffered, but Les did quite frequently and I'm sure his batting affected it. When both batting and keeping wicket, a player arches his back. Les did both for such long periods, I'm sure his problems can only have been made worse. That is why I really got my head down and tried to score runs only when the situation demanded. If we had, say, 400 runs or more on the board, I would go in and have a bit of fun, maybe playing to the gallery.

Although I made my debut in 1939, my career did not begin in earnest until after the War. My first two or three games before the War had been as a batsman, but I did get the chance of keeping wicket in the same side as Les, who was just one of ten other fielders. I shall be forever grateful for the words of encouragement Les and Kent captain Brian Valentine gave me during that first match as a 'keeper against Derbyshire at Gravesend. Norman Harding, our fast bowler who died at the age of 31 when he contracted infantile paralysis, nipped one back, Derbyshire captain Robin Buckston got an inside edge and I managed to hold the catch plunging to my left. Both Les and Brian came up to me and said: 'Well, Godfrey, what a marvellous catch to start your career with. You won't take many better, no matter how long you play. Well done!' Imagine the pride I felt hearing this from my heroes. That was not necessarily the best catch of my career – I think there was one at Scarborough that stands out more – but it gave me an immediate feeling of confidence.

I had met Les during my time on the Kent staff before the War, and I always felt a sense of awe in his presence in those early days. After the War, however, we soon became close friends. We had plenty in common: cricket, our love of parties and a good time and a round of golf. Our mutual love of golf provides the background to a story that illustrates the true professionalism of Les Ames.

We were playing Glamorgan at Swansea in 1949. The Welsh county were a marvellous side just after the War – they won the County Championship in 1948 – and shot us out for 49. Glamorgan replied with 319, and it looked as though the match would be over in two days. It suddenly dawned on Les and myself that the Open golf championship was in progress at Sandwich. We were both members at Deal, which was just down the road, so we decided to book out of our hotel and drive through the night in time to watch play at Sandwich the following day.

Les almost ruined our plans. When he went out in Kent's second innings, Les made a superb 69 on a turning pitch. He was not dismissed until near the end of the second day and Glamorgan won by ten wickets just before the close. I will never forget it. I was thinking that here we are, booked out of our hotel so we can watch the Open tomorrow, and Les is doing his damnedest to prolong the match into the third day. It could easily have meant that we missed our day's golf – although we had no chance of saving the game. Les, though, was such a professional and, of course, cricket came before golf.

We did make it to Sandwich, and saw Bobby Locke win the Open. Les and I both noticed – and I have often wondered if anybody else did – that Locke should have been disqualified. Locke marked his ball on the 18th green, but re-placed it in the wrong spot. He sank the putt, and no doubt would have done so from the correct position, but the fact remains that quite accidentally he had broken the rules.

Les and myself certainly enjoyed some lively times after the day's play had ended. There was one occasion when we were called before the Kent secretary to explain why the team was no longer welcome to stay at the Grand Hotel in Bristol. After a hard day, we had had a few drinks in the evening, becoming a little rowdy in the bar, and apparently had disturbed the peace of a few people's evenings. We were, of course, fit professional sportsmen and able to 'sweat off' the previous night's excesses, but occasionally they landed us in trouble.

No matter how unaffected we felt the following morning, it was important that those of us who had been drinking should work especially hard. Then nobody could point an accusing finger in our direction. Most cricketers like a beer after the day's play. Indeed, it helped us relax and, unless we really overdid it, probably enhanced our performance the next day. If a player does not enjoy himself, his concentration is often affected and, as a result, his performance deteriorates. I'm not saying we were alcoholics or anything as drastic as that; we just liked a good time.

There was one occasion when Les, a magnificent athlete

even towards the end of his career, was anxious to cross the road. Unfortunately, a taxi blocked his way, so instead of walking round it Les leaped straight over the top of this cab!

Another occasion I remember well was a party in Gloucester in 1948. Brian Valentine, in his last season with Kent, and B. O. Allen, the Gloucestershire captain, were there with Les and myself. Brian, who had had a drink or two, was fooling about and lunged at me with his fists. I had been a professional boxer before the War, and I easily swayed out of the way. Brian fell forward and struck his forehead on the mantelpiece, and there was blood spurting all over the place. Brian was about to start fighting when Les, ever the diplomat, grabbed him and insisted that it was his fault that he had hurt himself. The wound required stitches, and Brian, of course, was full of remorse the following morning.

Yes, we certainly had plenty of fun in those days, travelling round the country and socialising with other counties' players, whom we got to know very well. Maybe we overdid it slightly in Brian's final season, but it was all fairly harmless – or at least we thought so. There was one memorable occasion when we were at an hotel, and not only were we unable to get a drink but Brian was also asked to be quiet. Promptly he asked how much the hotel was worth. '£50,000,' came the reply. Brian, totally deadpan, removed his chequebook from his jacket and began to write a cheque for the amount. Fortunately, he apologised the next morning and the 'purchase' was forgotten.

4

Alan Knott, Bob Taylor and Rodney Marsh

THE THREE outstanding wicket-keepers of the modern generation have undoubtedly been Alan Knott, Bob Taylor and Rodney Marsh, not necessarily in that order. Although comparing 'keepers from different eras is a hazardous occupation, I have always maintained that Don Tallon is the finest I have seen. Knott, Taylor and Marsh, though, can rightly be discussed in the same breath.

Knott would almost certainly be the most capped cricketer in Test history but for his involvement with World Series Cricket and the rebel tour to South Africa. For years he was selected for England ahead of Taylor because of his superior ability with the bat. He has scored more Test runs than any other England wicket-keeper – including Les Ames, who admittedly played in less than half as many matches – and his total of more than 4,300 includes five centuries. He has reached three figures more times than any other stumper apart from Ames and Clyde Walcott, who did not keep throughout his career. Some might also claim Rohan Kanhai or even Viv Richards – both of whom have occasionally donned the gloves – were 'keepers who exceeded Knott's number of centuries.

'Knotty's' Test batting average of 32.75 is very respectable and higher than, among others, such famous names as Trevor Bailey, M. J. K. Smith, Roy McLean, Wilf Rhodes, Jim Parks, Richie Benaud and Vinoo Mankad.

Statistics alone do not fully indicate Alan's value to England over the years. Like so many of the best players, he rose to a challenge and usually batted better for England than for Kent. He was especially useful in a crisis. Coming in in the lower middle order, Knotty frequently saved

England and could combine a rock-like defence with impro-
vised attack. He had an instinct for survival, together with
enormous powers of concentration on one hand, with a
flair that allowed him to score very rapidly at times on the
other. He was the man who carted the great Indian spinners all over the field, just when they were imposing a
stranglehold on the other England batsmen, and, against
Lillee and Thomson in the winter of 1974–75, Knotty was
England's second highest scorer. His unorthodox style –
with the palm of the top hand facing towards the bowler –
is not to be recommended to youngsters, but it has served
Alan well over the years.

I believe it is entirely appropriate to go into Knott's
batting ability in such detail, because it was the reason he
was consistently chosen ahead of Bob Taylor for England.
Indeed, many people have always maintained that Bob was
the superior 'keeper. Knott, though, remains one of the
best stumpers in history.

His passion for physical fitness – manifested by his
famous on-field callisthenics – allows him to keep as well
now as when he first switched from being an off-spinner to
a wicket-keeper two decades ago. Alan has a wonderful
pair of hands and a great gift for anticipation. Some of his
keeping has been out of this world, especially when standing back. I have often criticised him for standing back when
the bowling has not really been fast enough to warrant it.
His answer is: 'Godfrey, I'm not as strongly built as you
were. I don't think I would be able, over a period of time, to
stand up without suffering injury of some kind. I also catch
more batsmen and let through fewer byes by standing
back.' There could be nothing worse than forcing Knotty to
go up to the stumps, when he would feel happier standing
back. Anyway, he has spent thousands of overs up to the
stumps taking Derek Underwood's bowling, which is no
easy task.

Alan Knott, the impish genius, made his Test debut in
1967 – taking seven catches against Pakistan at Trent
Bridge – and Bob Taylor, the perennial deputy, was per-
mitted only one Test appearance until Knott went to Packer
in 1977. Since then, Taylor, apart from brief spells by Knott

himself, Paul Downton and David Bairstow of Yorkshire, has held the Test place virtually unchallenged. Inferior wicket-keepers, allegedly better with the bat, have been used in one-day internationals, but with scant success.

Bob is not as good a batsman as Knott or Marsh, but he is determined and he has a frustrating knack (for bowlers, that is) of sticking around just when the fielding side needs a wicket. A couple of performances stand out. In Adelaide in 1978–79, Taylor (97) and his Derbyshire team-mate Geoff Miller added 135 for the seventh wicket – more than doubling the England score – and rescued their country when it looked as though Australia might win a low-scoring match. *Wisden* said: 'Certainly it was Taylor's innings of his life.' Another occasion when Taylor showed his tenacity with the bat was at Edgbaston in 1981. He scored 54 and with Bob Willis (28 not out) added a record for England against Pakistan of 79 for the tenth wicket. England won by 113 runs.

There could have been no higher compliment than the England selectors' decision to choose Taylor as the only wicket-keeper for the tour of Fiji, New Zealand and Pakistan in early 1984. Personally, I disagreed with the decision – what if Taylor became sick or injured? – but it was testimony to his fitness and talent that a man of 42 should be thought capable of handling all the wicket-keeping duties during an arduous three-month tour.

Before he left for that tour of Fiji, New Zealand and Pakistan, Bob was telling me that he did not mind being the only 'keeper in the party. 'It means that I will get more games,' was his reaction. He has not lost his enthusiasm for cricket and I know for a fact he was punishing his body along runs around the hilly countryside where he lives. Taylor wanted to make sure he was in the physical condition necessary to undertake the tour. Nothing would have offended his pride more than the England team having to call for another 'keeper.

He has scarcely missed a match through injury or illness – and certainly not through being dropped by Derbyshire – in a career spanning more than 20 years. He is the most prolific wicket-keeper in first-class cricket history, and if somebody had ever charted the number of dropped catches or missed stumpings, Taylor's figures would compare favourably with anyone's.

Unobtrusive, consistent, athletic and still with enormous pride in his performance, Taylor has it in him to continue playing until the age of . . . well, maybe 50? He toured all over the world as Knott's deputy before he finally received his chance and nobody begrudged him it. He is a kind and modest man, and not many cricketers have fewer enemies.

Taylor, the perfectionist, even gave up the Derbyshire captaincy because he feared the extra responsibility was affecting his wicket-keeping, although nobody else had noticed a decline. His footwork, handling and concentration cannot be faulted. Bob Taylor is one of my favourite cricketers.

Rod Marsh, when he started his career in Australia, was nicknamed 'Iron Gloves' because the ball bounced out of his hands so often. Times have changed. Marsh has made more dismissals than any other 'keeper in Test history – more than 350 – and he combined with Dennis Lillee to form the most successful of all fielder-bowler partnerships. The proliferation of Australian pace bowlers has meant that an unusually low number of Marsh's dismissals have been stumped. But that is not to say he is not an expert at standing up when the bowling demands it.

Marsh, a powerfully-built man who resembles a shambling bear, nonetheless has lightning reflexes and excellent judgement when diving. His determined, no-nonsense approach to cricket I'm sure inspires some of his teammates. And, if the batsman feels uncomfortable facing the likes of Lillee and Jeff Thomson, Rodney certainly does nothing to make them feel more at home. He, like most Australians, plays the game hard and to win.

His nickname changed from 'Iron Gloves' to 'Bacchus'. Asked why this was, Marsh replied: 'When a fielder threw the ball in, I always shouted "Back us up." ' Marsh, perhaps a little overweight at the start of his career, became even more determined to succeed when he heard those early criticisms.

He became the first wicket-keeper to score a century for

Alan Knott, Bob Taylor and Rodney Marsh

Australia in Test cricket. He can frustrate bowlers with solid defence, but will be best remembered for his ability to hit with thunderous power. His century in the Centenary Test at Melbourne in March 1977 was a memorable innings.

5

Cricket Can be Fun

WHEN I arrived late for a lesson and my chemistry master asked where I had been, I replied: 'I've been playing cricket on the far side of the field.'

'That's no good for you, Godfrey. You'll never earn your living from playing cricket,' came his earnest response.

From that day, I realised cricket and cricket stories could be fun. My opinion has never changed. Everybody who has ever played the game at any level has a wealth of cricketing yarns and I would like to share a few of my favourites. No sport attracts 'characters' with quite the same unerring regularity as cricket.

There was even a hint of farce about my trial at Canterbury, when I was looking to make my way in the game. The nets had been erected at an angle and, as a result, all the bowlers kept delivering balls down the legside. It was not much use to them or the batsmen, but it gave me the opportunity to show I was adept at taking down the legside.

Many memories are associated with 'firsts'. Like my first catch in county cricket – when my picture appeared in the paper the following day with me at full stretch and my mouth wide open. Then there was Fred Ridgway's first bouncer to Don Bradman – it disappeared into the tent by the boundary and Les Ames said: 'Imagine what we had to put up with when Don was a young man.'

I always maintained that when my powers began to diminish I would retire. Consequently, when, in my fortieth year, my reactions started to slow, I called it a day. However, I was determined to retain an involvement in cricket. This has happened by playing for teams such as the

International Cavaliers, Lord's Taverners and the Courage
Old England XI and through journalism and bookmaking.

The International Cavaliers, or plain Cavaliers as they
became known, were made up from former Test and county cricketers, retired but still highly proficient, and from
talented youngsters. So Ted Dexter and Denis Compton
might be in the same side as Alan Knott and Keith Fletcher,
who, of course, were just beginning their careers in the
sixties. We raised money for a beneficiary by playing
against his county on a Sunday in a televised match. It
proved an enormous success. Indeed, the Cavaliers
matches blazed the trail for the John Player League. The
authorities realised the potential of a match started and
finished on a Sunday afternoon, found a sponsor, and the
League was born.

The Lord's Taverners matches form a bond of friendship
between cricketers and show-business personalities. So,
for example, Eric Sykes will keep wicket to Alec Bedser.

'Stand up to the wicket like Godfrey does. It's quite easy,'
Alec will say.

Eric, somewhat sheepishly, moves up to the stumps and,
of course, the next ball goes for four byes.

'Never mind, Eric, perhaps you had better go back to
where you were.'

I particularly enjoy keeping wicket to the bowling of Tim
Brooke-Taylor, whose imitation of a fast bowler resembles a
broken-down long-distance runner. Harry Secombe, too,
bowls with so much determination that you would think
the future of the Western world depended on him not
bowling a bad ball. But it is right that these men from other
spheres of entertainment should try their hardest when
playing cricket – they are raising money for charity.

When Peter Thomson, five times winner of the British
Open golf championship, came out to bat in one match, we
said: 'Okay lads, give him a chance – he does not play
cricket very much.' Peter was trying to hit every ball over
mid-wicket, with a swing similar to a hooked tee-shot. He
was dropped a couple of times (on purpose, of course), but
gradually began to play quite well, hitting the ball in the
middle of the bat until he had scored 30.

'Okay, Peter's had a good chance. But that's enough. We'll get him out now,' the word went round.

But we could not. Peter had his eye in and kept hitting the ball over the mid-wicket boundary and, by now, he was not offering any chances. He made an excellent century, receiving a standing ovation from both the crowd and players. To him, it must have been like a cricketer going out and shooting par round St Andrews. Peter could scarcely contain his grin and said: 'I should have been a cricketer, not a golfer.'

During the Centenary Test match celebrations in England in 1980, there was a nostalgic match at The Oval between Old England and Old Australia. There was Neil Harvey, who claimed he had not picked up a bat since he retired, rolling back the years with a series of glorious cover drives. I was more than 60 years old and handed over the gloves to Jim Parks halfway through the Australian innings, but not before I had made a couple of stumpings. The crowd gave me a generous ovation and I remember one chap saying: 'Godfrey, you're just as good as ever you were.' Which reminds me.

We were taking part in the film *The Final Test* and Len Hutton, our captain, had to say: 'Don't worry, you're just as good as ever you were.' Len was unhappy with the line and kept repeating it to himself. So much so that one night Len woke up and said aloud: 'Don't worry, you are just as good as ever you were.'

His wife, Dorothy, stirred and muttered: 'Darling, I wish I could say the same about you!'

The success of the Old England v. Old Australia match prompted the thought that it would be a good idea if the retired players could play regularly. So, under the sponsorship of Courage, the Old England XI now have a fairly extensive fixture list, playing teams all over the country for charity.

Our captain, Fred Trueman, ever the entertainer, makes the presentations after the games in which he plays, and his stories have the spectators and participants in raptures. I know the old players enjoy the opportunity to play in a fairly competitive atmosphere and, certainly, the teams we play are very determined and enjoy the chance to boast: 'I hit Fred Trueman for four' or 'I took a catch to dismiss Tom Graveney.' The ex-England lads renew acquaintances, recall stories and the general camaraderie in the dressing-room is delightful. We are able to raise some money for charity and, what's more, we get paid for it.

I also wrote a column for a Sunday newspaper, and my involvement with Ladbrokes began in the unlikely setting of a swimming pool in Jamaica. We were on a Cavaliers' tour and were invited to a magnificent house overlooking Montego Bay. It was the residence of William Hill, the famous bookmaker. I was chatting to him and Colin Ingleby-Mackenzie and mentioned that I had always been interested in betting on cricket. Did William think there was a market for it in England?

'That's a good idea, Godfrey,' he said, 'I will give you £10,000 to try to get it started. Let me know how you get on.'

I enquired whether it might be possible to start the operation in Kent, but was met with a series of blank expressions. So the project was temporarily abandoned. At least, William had not lost his £10,000.

A couple of years later, Colin rang me to say that, if I was still interested in betting on cricket, I should meet him for lunch in the Ladbroke Club in Hill Street. Ladbrokes had decided to enter the field of cricket bookmaking and asked Colin to be their adviser. He had been forced to turn down their offer because of other commitments, but recommended me instead. I was introduced to Ron Pollard, the man in charge of Ladbroke's cricket betting. We had a highly convivial lunch and since that day I have been the company's adviser on cricket betting. There are several ways of trying to beat the punters – not just who will win the match, but the number of wickets to fall or runs scored in one particular session, who will be the highest-scoring batsman in the match, and so on. You can just imagine the tension involved when a man has bet that between 101 and 110 runs will be scored before lunch and the final over of the morning begins with, say, 97 on the board. Cricket betting, for me, is fun.

Not so long ago I was asked whether I had ever disputed an umpire's decision – an ugly feature that is becoming too common these days – and, somewhat ashamedly, I had to admit that I had. Just once. It was during the Scarborough Festival and the late Alec Skelding, perhaps the most famous of all umpires, had been taken ill during the afternoon's play. One of the lads from the local cricket club took his place.

Johnny Wardle was performing his tricks with the ball from the Pavilion End. Eric Bedser, the batsman, moved down the pitch to one of Johnny's well-flighted chinamen. The ball pitched middle and leg and Eric, attempting to hit it over mid-wicket, played a 'walking shot', in which the right foot is forced up the pitch by the swing of the body. I removed the bails and shouted 'Howzat?' To my astonishment – and everybody else's – the new umpire rejected my appeal.

It was such a dreadful decision that, at the end of the over, I told the umpire what I thought of him. Although this was a Festival match, the cricket was being taken seriously, and I believe the public – especially in Yorkshire – want to watch authentic matches. Anyway, at the tea interval, the Scarborough secretary found another replacement umpire and our friend left the ground, never to be seen again. I was clearly wrong to question his decision in such an animated manner. After all, he was only doing his best and, I expect, was overawed by the occasion.

Another story concerning umpires took place at Lord's during a Gentlemen v. Players match. My dear friend Sam Pothecary, the ex-Hampshire player, was umpiring at square leg, when I completed a quick stumping down the legside off a Doug Wright googly. But Sam said: 'Not out.' At the end of the over, I waited for Sam to come to the wicket and said: 'Sam, I thought I made a good stumping.'

'Well, Godfrey, you may well have done. But, quite honestly, you woke me up. I was thinking about the wife's sister and by the time I had my wits about me, the batsman's foot was behind the crease. I had no option but to give it not out. I'm sorry.'

How could I be angry with such an honest reply? I just burst out laughing.

Joe Hardstaff, the elegant batsman from Nottinghamshire, was a man who featured in a number of good stories. One match, in which I was not playing, was between Middlesex and Nottinghamshire. Joe forced Jim Sims through the covers off the back foot, pushed off strongly with his left foot and shouted: 'Two.' But his back foot slipped, touched the stumps and dislodged a bail. Joe, renowned for his unwillingness to surrender his wicket, realised what had happened and on the second run ran straight at the wicket, knocking over the stumps and charging into Fred Price, the Middlesex wicket-keeper who had been trying to attract the umpire's attention to the errant bail. Poor Fred ended flat on his back. Joe was given not out and Fred, who had quite a stutter, was heard to say: 'Joe, you're a fl..fl..fli..fli..flipping cheat.'

I was batting with Joe during a Test match at Barbados in 1947–48. He played superbly until he reached 98. Then he got stuck. I had the bowling and dispatched a half-volley from Foffie Williams to the boundary. When we passed each other, Joe said: 'You lucky blighter, Godfrey. I wish he would bowl one of those to me.' Soon afterwards, Joe received a similar delivery from the same bowler and was bowled for 98.

On another occasion, Kent were playing Nottinghamshire at Canterbury. Notts, batting last on a turning pitch, had no chance of victory and were keen to catch the 3.30 train home . . . it was before the War when travelling was not as easy as nowadays. Joe went in to bat, intending to have a go and get out, so the team could get to the station in time. They caught the train all right: Joe swung the bat at everything, scored the fastest century of the season in 51 minutes and Nottinghamshire won the match.

Another one of the greatest innings I saw was inspired by outside influences. Whereas Joe Hardstaff's was prompted by the desire to catch a train, Denis Compton's was the result of a comment from his captain.

Middlesex were a side I enjoyed playing against. Their boys always had a drink after the day's play and the repartee between Jack Young and Denis Compton was something I certainly did not want to miss. Denis, of course, was a mighty player and I remember one match when Kent left Middlesex a decidedly unlikely target on the last day. Denis was a little upset because the Kent captain, Brian Valentine, was making the task even more difficult by placing the fielders on the boundary. When Walter Robins, the Middlesex skipper, came out to bat he said: 'Denis, there appears to be no chance. I think we'll shut up shop and play out time.'

'You're right, skipper. All the fielders are out – there's no chance,' replied Denis.

After a further three or four overs, I could see Denis was becoming frustrated. 'These bloody fielders all out on the boundary,' he said to me. 'Come on, Godfrey, tell your captain to give us a chance.'

'You're the batsman, Denis, it is up to you to make the first move,' I said.

Suddenly, Denis shouted down the pitch at Walter: 'Skipper, I can't stand this. I'm going to give it a go.'

'It's all yours,' was Robins's reply, and there was a smile on his face as he spoke.

I have wondered to this day whether Walter's first words to Denis when he came out to bat were spoken with a purpose. He knew Denis had the ability to win the match and that, by urging him to play for a draw, he would arouse his instinct for a challenge. Compton was eventually caught at cover off Doug Wright for 168. Denis's knock was breathtaking.

A number of stories surround Charlie Harris, that fine Nottinghamshire batsman who, somewhat surprisingly, never played for England. Charlie was a dedicated professional and also a bit of a wag. When he came out to bat he used to say: 'Good morning, fellow workers.' And when he later became an umpire, Charlie would take the bails off at the close of play and say: 'And that concludes the entertainment for today, gentlemen.'

I remember one match against Nottinghamshire that was fizzling out into a tame draw. With one over to go, I was facing Charlie on 97 not out. Les Ames was at the other end having scored 140 odd. The only interest left was whether or not I would complete my century. Charlie said: 'If that young bugger wants a century, he'll have to earn it.'

I hit the first ball to fine leg and tried for two runs, but Les, quite rightly, stopped me. I had to settle for a single. Les came up to me and said: 'I'll get a single and then you have four balls to get your century.' Charlie then proceeded to bowl his next four balls as far away from the stumps as possible. They were all close to being wides – one delivery went for four byes – and Les was unable to get that single. I was left 98 not out.

On another occasion, during the War, Charlie Harris, who was in the army at Woolwich, was selected to play at Lord's for a game against a Dominion side. People had been starved of cricket for so long and there was a full house. Charlie scored a superb century before lunch. In the evening, when the players put in their expenses claims for travelling to the match, Charlie charged ten shillings for his journey from Woolwich. When he received his expenses, he had been paid 3s 6d, which was the exact fare. Charlie was again selected for the next match at Lord's. Another full house. At lunch, Charlie was 28 not out. During the interval, 'Plum' Warner, who had organised the game, said: 'What are you doing, Charlie? The bowling is not very good, so why are you scoring so slowly?'

Said Charlie: 'Thou gets what thou bloody well pays for!'

The lighter side is an essential ingredient of professional cricket. People are out on the field for hours on end, often amid enormous tension, and a form of release is required. Even some cricketers, perhaps with a reputation for being slightly more straitlaced, joined in. Did you ever notice Colin Cowdrey mimicking other cricketers? He often did Denis Compton after the knee operation – complete with the distinct rolling gait, a little knock-kneed, loose arms hanging from the shoulders, and the hands gesticulating as if to say: 'What's going on?'

Ken Barrington was another great mimic. Colin and Ken would walk down the wicket between overs, each with his left shoulder higher than his right, with left elbow pointing outwards and upwards and with a hand holding the peak of his cap. They were impersonating Tom Graveney.

Tom was – indeed still is – a great watcher of cricket. Before he went in to bat, he sat and watched every second of the game, analysing every aspect of it. This came naturally to Tom, although many cricketers found it tiresome. He familiarised himself with all field placings and what the bowlers were doing, so that he would know what to expect when he went out. Personally, I hardly ever watched the game before I went in to bat. My best performances were usually when somebody woke me up as a wicket fell and it was my turn to bat. Mind you, I was always dressed, with pads on and bat and gloves at the ready.

Superstitions were an important part of some players' games. Ken Barrington, for instance, always put on his left sock first and Denis Compton's left pad went on before his right. Denis was so absent-minded, though, that he sometimes went out to bat without wearing a box.

Ken Barrington loved batting. I was given a good example of this near the start of his career when Kent were playing at The Oval. Surrey needed just a few more runs to complete an easy victory. I had asked my captain if I could field and not keep wicket, so, when Ken was batting with two runs to win, I was fielding at mid-wicket. He rocked back and hammered a short-pitched ball hard about a foot above my head. I stuck up a hand, hoping it would not make contact because the ball was going so fast. But it thumped into the upper half of my hand, bounced up about three feet and I dived and caught the rebound. Ken was livid: 'What did you do that for, Godfrey? You've spoilt my average.'

'I've got to show the lads I can catch when I'm not wearing my gloves,' I replied.

'Quite right, Godfrey. Shame you had to choose me to prove it,' countered Kenny with a broad grin.

Graham Gooch is the modern Mike Yarwood. He has an extensive repertoire of impersonations of other bowlers and, along with characters such as Ray East, helps to make Essex probably the most humorous of all the seventeen county sides. Their antics ensure a relaxed atmosphere on the field and in the dressing-room, a principal reason for Essex's success in recent seasons, I'm sure.

I mentioned the Lord's Taverners earlier in this chapter, but those are not the only matches in which cricketers past and present play against men from other fields of entertainment. I remember playing at Petersfield, a picturesque ground in Hampshire, for a World of Sport XI, captained by John Bromley, now Independent Television's Head of Sport. Dickie Davies was bowling his seamers with considerable pace, when the batsman took a mighty swing, missed, lost his balance and I took off the bails. Dickie could not believe it. 'I'll tear this page out of the scorebook and put it in a frame in my front room,' he said. 'Stumped Evans, bowled Davies.' Dickie rewarded me by pouring an especially large gin into my glass, topping it up with tonic and saying: 'Even if it never happens again, Godders, I can claim for the rest of my life that Godfrey Evans made a stumping of my bowling. You are my friend for life!'

6

Wicket-keeper Batsmen

FIFTY YEARS ago, every team chose the best wicket-keeper available to go behind the stumps. Today it is not so simple. Many sides – including England – have selected men to keep wicket on the strength of their batting. Alan Knott was for years given preference over Bob Taylor because he had more run-scoring potential. There was little to choose between their wicket-keeping. In more recent times, men such as David Bairstow and Ian Gould have got in ahead of Taylor, even though they were inferior wicket-keepers.

This policy would have been still more foolhardy before the War, when there was such a diversity of bowling in every side. Nowadays, 'keepers spend maybe 80 per cent of their time standing back, mainly to bowlers little above medium-pace, which makes the 'keeper's job less difficult. So team captains often decide to foresake the risk of a missed chance for extra run-scoring potential, especially in one-day cricket.

Wicket-keepers expected to be able to bat are not the only participants whose role has changed over the years. Bowlers were not really expected to chase the ball across the outfield as such exertion put unreasonable demands on their stamina. This was accepted as the duty of the batsmen of the side when they were fielding. Now, of course, the level of fitness has improved beyond recognition and a fast bowler would be expected to make, say, two or three substantial chases between overs during a spell. Also in the old days, when his side batted, a bowler used to go in and swing the bat. A little bit of fun for them and the spectators, really. Only if a few runs were required for victory, or for extra points in the Championship, would a bowler really get his head down.

Personally, I would always pick the best wicket-keeper available. Batting would come into it only if the two 'keepers were of equal ability behind the stumps. Over the years, though, there have been plenty of men who, quite apart from being outstanding wicket-keepers, have also been able to bat a bit. They are the wicket-keeper batsmen.

Les Ames, my cricketing hero and the best wicket-keeper batsman of them all, merits an entire chapter to himself. But Les is by no means the only man who has been hugely proficient with both gloves and bat.

Edward Tylecote, of Oxford University and Kent, was perhaps the first genuine wicket-keeper batsman. As a 'keeper he was one of the first men to do away with longstops. He scored a century for the Gentlemen against the Players in 1883, and another of his finest innings was a not out hundred for Kent against the 1882 Australians at Canterbury. Jack Board of Gloucestershire, who played six times for England, passed 1,000 runs in a season on six occasions and Surrey's Henry Wood averaged 68 in his four Test matches. The two great Warwickshire 'keepers around the turn of the century – Dick Lilley and 'Tiger' Smith – played a combined total of 46 Test matches for England. Lilley averaged more than 20 with the bat for England and registered 16 centuries during his first-class career. Smith scored 20 centuries.

George Brown of Hampshire scored 37 first-class centuries, yet even that outstanding ability as a wicket-keeper batsman could not guarantee him a regular place in the England side. He played just seven Test matches in the early 1920s – a period when England were blessed with a wealth of batting talent.

George Duckworth, allegedly the better 'keeper, was initially chosen ahead of Les Ames for England. Les, who scored 102 first-class centuries during his career, was clearly a vastly superior batsman. 'Duckie', who was famous for his loud appeal, was a magnificent stumper, but he averaged just 14.62 with the bat in Test cricket. When Duckie's best days were over, Ames made the England job virtually his own up until the Second World War and scored eight Test centuries in 47 matches, an outstanding record for a specialist batsman, let alone one who also had to concentrate on his wicket-keeping duties.

There were others who played for England during this era. Like the amazing Harry Elliott from Derbyshire, who made 194 consecutive appearances for his county, enjoyed a brief Test career of just four matches and then returned to county cricket to play a further unbroken run of 232 matches for Derbyshire. Bill Farrimond of Lancashire toured both South Africa and the West Indies with MCC and was a better batsman than Duckworth, but he played only four Test matches before the outbreak of War – mainly because, by then, Ames was firmly entrenched in the England team.

Fred Price of Middlesex, known as 'The Rock of Gibraltar' because of his stubborn defence and short backlift, played in just one Test – against Australia at Headingley in 1938. Price equalled the then world record of seven catches in an innings for Middlesex against Yorkshire in 1937. Arthur Wood of Yorkshire was another who represented England four times – and one of those games was against Australia at The Oval in 1938. England scored the little matter of 903 for seven, the highest total in Test history, to which Len Hutton contributed 364. Wood, possessor of the honed wit common to so many Yorkshiremen, went in when the score was 770 for six and, as he walked down the pavilion steps, he was heard to say: 'Eh, just t'man for a crisis!'

Paul Gibb, who played for Yorkshire and later for Essex, was selected for England as both a specialist batsman and wicket-keeper. He toured South Africa in 1938–39 – the last England tour before the War – and in that series scored two centuries and was dismissed in the nineties in another innings. Paul's Test batting average in his eight England appearances was 44.69 – which compares remarkably well with his first-class career figure of 28.

In 1945, I was selected for an England XI against the Combined Services for the Victory Tests. But I was stationed in Germany at the time and my commanding officer would not allow me to play. So Billy Griffith of Sussex made the team. Billy was an excellent 'keeper, but will probably be best remembered for his century against the West Indies in Trinidad in 1947–48. He opened the batting with Jack Robertson in a side ravaged by injury. Jack was our one outstanding batsman but, in the first innings, Billy ran him out in the first over. There can seldom have been a more determined effort to compensate for an error. Billy batted all day in intense heat, scored his maiden century in first-class cricket and was eventually dismissed for 140. Time and again, Billy had to pause between deliveries because of spasms of cramp in his hands and legs – an indication of just how much perspiration he shed during his marathon effort. (Those salt tablets came in useful, you know!) Billy was another whose Test batting average was markedly superior to that in the first-class game – 31.40 against 16.42. Billy was the only 'keeper who went with me on more than one overseas tour with MCC.

Of the others, Dick Spooner was perhaps the best bats-man. Dick, an opener, had a career batting average of 27, made more than 1,000 runs in a season on six occasions and scored a dozen centuries. Brian Taylor, a particularly strong offside player, was nicknamed 'Foghorn' because his loud voice carried so far, and also 'Tonker' because he hit the ball very hard.

Arthur McIntyre, Keith Andrew and Roy Swetman each in turn accompanied me on my three tours of Australia. Of the trio, Arthur was the best batter and, indeed, played in the 1950–51 series as a batsman, although he did not come off. Roy, a short man, made some useful Test scores and averaged 16.93 in his eleven matches. Roy's quickness of foot and method of keeping his hands close to his body and jumping into position at the last moment made him almost unique. But I have always maintained that if a player has a style that works for him – and remember Roy's lack of inches presented him with problems all of his own when batting – there is no reason why he should alter it.

By the sixties, Tony Lock and Jim Laker had finished their careers and, as a result, the wicket-keepers spent more time standing back. During this era, there were three wicket-keepers all of whom played for England and all of whom could bat exceptionally well – Alan Smith, John Murray and Jim Parks.

Alan, now secretary of Warwickshire, the county he played for, and England manager on the winter tour of 1983–84, was an astonishing all-round cricketer. He once took a hat-trick of Essex wickets with his medium-pacers. Mind you, Alan is not the only wicket-keeper to have performed the hat-trick. There was a certain T. G. Evans who once captured three wickets in as many balls in that famous cricketing land of Kuwait!

John Murray, elegance personified, was a marvellously graceful batsman. He looked particularly impressive when driving through the covers or using his power to hit over long-on. JT, the most prolific wicket-keeper in first-class cricket history until Bob Taylor passed his figure of 1,527 dismissals, scored a Test century and finished his 21-match international career with the highly respectable average of 22.

Jim Parks played for England for his batting alone and, not until he took over the gloves in an emergency for Sussex (and performed so admirably that he kept the job) did he switch from being an outstanding cover point fieldsman and useful leg-spin bowler. Jim scored more than 50 centuries, in excess of 36,000 runs and finished with an average of 34. His greatest qualities were his footwork against spin bowling – he was always able to get to the pitch of the ball and smother the spin – and his delicate cuts and glides which were responsible for over 50 per cent of his runs off fast bowling. I believe that if Jim had taken up wicket-keeping earlier and he had had the opportunity to keep regularly to top-class spin bowling – remember Sussex never possessed quality slow bowlers during Jim's career – he could have been a truly outstanding 'keeper. As it is, I still consider Parks to be the second finest of all wicket-keeper batsmen behind Les Ames.

Geoff Millman opened the batting for Nottinghamshire on several occasions and had a good record as a wicket-keeper, but business commitments cut short his career. Alan Knott and Bob Taylor are discussed in another chapter. Roger Tolchard, that fine wicket-keeper batsman from

Leicestershire, is another who deserves praise. He played in only four Test matches – and then as a specialist batsman – in an era dominated by Knott and Taylor, but his career encompassed more than 15,000 runs and in excess of 1,000 victims. He helped make Leicestershire one of the outstanding county sides of the 1970s and his running between the wickets was a lesson for many others. Of the current generation, the men likely to take over when Taylor does eventually call it a day – and goodness knows when that might be! – none is an exceptional batsman. Jack Richards of Surrey, a highly competent 'keeper who has been known to stand up to the now retired Robin Jackman, has made a century in senior cricket, but is never likely to score as heavily as the likes of Ames, Parks or Knott. Ian Gould, whose 'keeping – especially standing up – is probably not quite good enough for the highest level, opens for Sussex in the John Player League and his aggressive instincts with the bat are well suited to the one-day game. Bruce French of Nottinghamshire, and Hampshire's Bobby Parks, the son of Jim, are both highly promising 'keepers, but little more than staunch batsmen at the moment. Paul Downton opened the batting for Middlesex with some success after leaving Kent, before dropping down the order.

Now for a few words about outstanding wicket-keeper batsmen from other countries.

AUSTRALIA

Billy Murdoch, a close friend of W. G. Grace and one of the principal figures in the early cricket history of Australia, was an outstanding batsman who sometimes donned the gloves. Murdoch once held the record first-class score outside England of 321 and was the first man to score a Test double century. His first-class career included 20 centuries. He kept wicket in one of his 18 Tests for Australia and in the second innings of the single Test he played for England. Jack Blackham and James Kelly, who played in 35 and 36 Tests for Australia and averaged 15 and 17 respectively,

I kept wicket to Doug Wright on hundreds of occasions. He had a high, bounding approach and action and his seven first-class hat-tricks is a world record. *The Photo Source*

Left: H.B. 'Jock' Cameron of South Africa, an outstanding international wicket-keeper between the wars, batting during the 1935 series in England. Les Ames, the best wicket-keeper batsman of all time, is behind. *The Photo Source*

Right: Brian Valentine, the Kent captain after the War, was an excellent skipper and a man with whom I had a lot of fun. *The Photo Source*

Below: Keith Miller, Denis Compton, Bill Edrich and myself during Keith's *This is Your Life* programme, recorded in Australia at the time of the Centenary Test in March 1977.

Far left: With Denis Compton so far down the pitch, this was probably not the most difficult stumping I completed in my career! But getting rid of the great man was always a little special. This game was at Lord's in 1957, Denis's last full season, and Kent won by an innings and 59 runs. Denis, though, scored a half century in each innings. The next highest scorer for Middlesex in the match was Bill Edrich, with a combined total in two innings of 36. *S & G Press Agency Ltd*

Left: Deryck Murray who spent much of his Test career handling the battery of West Indies fast bowlers. *Adrian Murrell/Allsport Photographic*

Above: Wasim Bari, one of the outstanding wicket-keepers of the world in recent years and the first Pakistani to complete 200 dismissals in Test cricket, about to catch Allan Lamb off Sikander Bakht during the Edgbaston Test match in 1982. *Adrian Murrell/Allsport Photographic*

Left: Farokh Engineer of India was a man who enjoyed his cricket. As wicket-keeper, some of his work on the legside when standing up to the stumps was superb. He also scored more than 2,500 runs in Test cricket. Farokh is pictured here during the Edgbaston Test match in 1974. The England batsman is David Lloyd, his Lancashire colleague, who scored 214 not out in this innings. *The Photo Source*

There have been few more determined competitors behind the stumps than Australia's Rodney Marsh. The most prolific wicket-keeper in Test history has just completed another dismissal during the 1982-83 series against England. Allan Lamb is the departing batsman.
Adrian Murrell/Allsport Photographic

Bob Taylor, for years the eternal deputy to Alan Knott but latterly England's undisputed first choice behind the stumps, is jubilant after stumping Greg Chappell off Derek Underwood in the Perth Test in January 1980. Mike Brearley is at slip. *Adrian Murrell/Allsport Photographic*

I still maintain Don Tallon is the finest wicket-keeper I have seen. Here I am caught behind by the great Australian off the bowling of Alan Davidson after scoring eight in the first Test at Trent Bridge in 1953. *The Photo Source*

Tattered and torn, but still Taylor's choice . . . Bob, like most wicket-keepers, is a man always reluctant to discard a favourite pair of gloves. Here he appeals unsuccessfully for an lbw decision against Kim Hughes, the Australian captain, during the Edgbaston Test in 1981.

Adrian Murrell/Allsport Photographic

could not be classed as exceptional at batting as well as wicket-keeping.

Their successor was Sammy Carter, whom I remember meeting in Sydney during the Test there in 1946–47. He was nearly 70 and in a wheelchair, but did not wear glasses despite his age. Bertie Oldfield introduced us and I can recall being surprised by Sammy's keenness and awareness of the game. His average of 22.97 in 28 Tests was presentable and he took part in the dismissal of 65 batsmen, 44 of them caught. That is a low proportion compared with figures these days, but during Carter's time 44 out of 65 was quite a substantial ratio of catches. The reason, simply, was that Carter preferred to stand back to the medium-pacers.

Next came the legendary Bertie Oldfield, an artist among wicket-keepers and probably the first 'keeper to design his own gauntlets. Fifty-two of his 130 victims in Test cricket were stumped, largely off the bowling of Clarrie Grimmett and Bill O'Reilly. Bertie had a very hot time during the 1932–33 Bodyline series. He retired hurt at Adelaide after being struck on the head by a Larwood bouncer – although Bertie admits it was his own fault – and that might have affected many people's confidence for life. Bertie's Test career average was 22.65, showing that he was certainly no mug with the bat and that he overcame the nightmarish experiences of bodyline bowling.

A whole string of excellent wicket-keepers followed Oldfield – Ben Barnett, Don Tallon, Gil Langley, Wally Grout, Brian Taber and Barry Jarman among them. None was an outstanding batsman but, then, Australia's batting was so strong that those extra runs from the 'keeper were not usually required. Then came Rodney Marsh, a pugnacious cricketer whose wicket-keeping improved through the years. As a left-handed batsman, Marsh is at his happiest attacking the bowling and has scored approaching 4,000 Test runs.

SOUTH AFRICA

South Africa, with its wonderful climate and good wickets, has produced a chain of cricketing talent and in it have been a number of fine wicket-keeper batsmen. Percy Sherwell, their captain, batted at nine, ten or eleven during the series against England in 1905–06. But, by the time he led the touring team to England in 1907, Sherwell was opening the batting for South Africa as well as keeping wicket. Sherwell scored a century at Lord's in 1907 and finished his 13-Test career with an average of 23.72. Sixteen of his 36 victims were stumpings, mainly off the great South African spin bowlers who pioneered the googly around the turn of the century, such as Bosanquet, Schwarz, Vogler and Faulkner. Tommy Ward was their next regular 'keeper and, despite a career interrupted by illness and injury, he played in 23 Tests, averaging a modest 13.90. Ward never settled in a regular place in the batting order – number ten one match and opening in the next – and he did score a couple of half centuries going in first.

Horace 'Jock' Cameron, who is considered by many to have been South Africa's finest wicket-keeper, could bat a bit, too. Although he never made a century, his Test average was 30.21 in 26 matches before his life was cut short by a rare fever. Les Ames often talked about Cameron's talent. Ronnie Grieveson played only two Tests, one of which was the 'timeless' match in Durban in 1938–39 which was abandoned as a draw after ten days because the England team had to begin their two-day rail journey back to the waiting ship in Cape Town. Grieveson scored 75 in that game and it was unfortunate the War ended his career. Billy Wade, who never toured with South Africa, made a century and averaged 28.38 in his eleven Tests.

The post-War period was dominated by Johnny Waite. He was the only South African to play in 50 Tests, scored four centuries and averaged 30.44. Johnny was remarkably nimble for a tall man and his height gave him a big extension when diving. Waite, who claimed 141 victims in Test cricket, was a quiet, honest man and extremely popular with team-mates and opposition. Denis Lindsay would

58

probably have got into the South African side on the strength of his batting alone – he scored three centuries in his 19 Tests, in addition to 57 catches and two stumpings. Russell Endean, a fine batsman, occasionally kept wicket, but not very soundly. There have been some fine wicket-keeper batsmen playing Currie Cup cricket in recent years and it is sad that they have not been able to exhibit their talents on a worldwide stage.

WEST INDIES

It is one of the strange facets of West Indian cricket that, alongside all the brilliant batsmen, fearsome fast bowlers, subtle spinners and fantastic fielders, there has never been a truly great wicket-keeper to emerge from the Caribbean. The best before the War was undoubtedly Ivan Barrow, who was principal wicket-keeper for the West Indies for almost a decade leading up to 1939 and yet, in those days of limited international cricket, played only eleven Tests. Barrow, who often opened the innings, scored a century against England at Old Trafford in 1933 and, together with George Headley, put on 200 for the second wicket. He claimed 22 victims.

The West Indies were hampered less by the War than, say, England – at least in a cricketing sense. Once Test cricket returned, they introduced three great cricketing talents from Barbados to the world game. The 'Three Ws' – Worrell, Weekes and Walcott – became great figures in the history of the game and Clyde Walcott, a 6 ft 2 in, 15-stone colossus of a man, was one of the best wicket-keepers in the business for a time. Nobody doubted his ability with the bat, for he scored 15 Test centuries, and his power of stroke was awesome. I remember when we landed in the West Indies for the start of the 1947–48 tour, and went straight to the Barbados ground for practice. There was Clyde in the middle, with no net and literally hundreds of youngsters throwing the ball at him as hard as they could. He was standing there, hammering it all over the ground.

'What do you think of him? He's one of our best players,' said one of the locals.

'He looks great,' I replied, 'but we have a bowler called Jim Laker, who could well trap him lbw with his off spinners.'

'No he won't,' came the reply. 'His uncle is umpiring.'

Clyde did not keep regularly throughout his career, but I can tell you he was magnificent behind the stumps. He had rapid reflexes, a huge reach and a safe pair of hands, and he finished with 64 dismissals in Test cricket. Clyde, as if to prove his versatility, was not a bad medium-pace bowler, either.

Gerry Alexander and Jackie Hendricks did the job for a number of years. Gerry, an aggressive batsman and astute captain, made one Test hundred, finished with an average of 30.03 and collected 90 victims. Jackie, a powerful man who played 20 times for his country, never made as many runs as his potential suggested and he finished with the disappointing average, for him, of 18.62.

Deryck Murray, a modest and likeable man, was the West Indies' first choice for a decade and most of his 189 victims were from catches taken off the great fast bowlers of his time. Deryck's 'keeping, rather like his batting, was solid rather than brilliant. He made several good scores when they were most needed on the rare occasions the mighty West Indian batting line-up failed.

Deryck's namesake David (no relation) scored a Test double century and the most recent West Indian stumper, Jeff Dujon, might yet become the best wicket-keeper batsman in Caribbean cricket history.

NEW ZEALAND

Not until some of the best New Zealand cricketers came to play in English county cricket did the Kiwis produce a side capable of threatening the best in the world. Nowadays, with men such as Richard Hadlee, Geoff Howarth and John Wright in the team, they pose a serious challenge to any country. Years ago, though, New Zealand were often a soft touch in Test cricket. With a small population and a climate that does not encourage good pitches, they struggled to unearth top-class cricketers.

Ken James was the first New Zealander to make inroads as a 'keeper but, although he scored seven first-class centuries, his Test average was a paltry 4.72. Frank Mooney, a solid 'keeper and useful run-getter who played in the immediate post-War period, and Eric Petrie each played 14 times for New Zealand. John Reid, with Hadlee the finest all-round cricketer in New Zealand history, often kept wicket, when he was not batting powerfully or bowling seam-up. Art Dick was a competent performer behind the sticks; he kept in 17 Tests (51 victims, batting average 14.23).

Perhaps New Zealand's finest wicket-keeper was Ken Wadsworth, who toured all the leading countries during his 33-match Test career. Ken's career came to a tragic end in 1976 when he died of cancer before the age of 30. He averaged 21.48 with the bat and established a New Zealand record of 96 dismissals. Jock Edwards, a somewhat roly-poly man, mighty hitter and fun cricketer, had a spell behind the stumps, but New Zealand's most regular 'keeper since Wadsworth has been Warren Lees, another useful batsman, who has registered a Test century.

INDIA

Most of the men behind the stumps for India before the War tended to concentrate too much on their batting and not enough on their wicket-keeping. As a result, the standard was not very high. Dilawar Hussain, for example, finished with a fine average of 42.33 in his admittedly short Test career of three matches. He claimed seven victims.

Dattaram Hindlekar opened the batting for India against England at Lord's in 1936 and, ten years later, saved a Test match at Old Trafford by surviving for 13 minutes on the final evening. Hindlekar's hands were rather brittle and he suffered from broken fingers throughout his career. Nana Joshi, Probir Sen and Narendra Tamhane, who played in

12, 14 and 21 Tests respectively, were in contention during the 1950s. Their next three principal wicket-keepers, who have served them until the present day, were all admirable performers with both gloves and bat – Budha Kunderan, Farokh Engineer and Syed Kirmani.

Kunderan played in 18 Tests and, in that time, scored two centuries and averaged 32.7. Engineer was a marvellously animated cricketer – a smile was rarely far from his face – and a good one, too. His 'keeping was sound and often brilliant down the legside when standing up. Farokh, during a 46-match Test career, scored a couple of centuries, 2,611 runs and averaged 31.08. His 82 dismissals were made up of 66 catches and 16 stumpings. Farokh's successor was another likeable character, Syed Kirmani. He must have learned a lot from Farokh, who, of course, gained plenty of experience himself playing English county cricket for Lancashire.

Kirmani, now India's most-capped 'keeper, is a consistent and resolute performer with the bat and a sparkling one behind the stumps. While Kapil Dev received most of the plaudits for leading India to victory in the 1983 Prudential World Cup, nobody appreciated more than the Indian captain the significance of Kirmani's contribution. He was superb and was deservedly named Gordon's Gin Wicket-keeper of the World Cup.

PAKISTAN

Imtiaz Ahmed, a fine wicket-keeper batsman, played in Pakistan's first 39 Test matches, including their memorable victory over England at The Oval in 1954 – the match in which I passed Bertie Oldfield's Test record of 130 dismissals. Imtiaz's three Test centuries included an innings of 209 against New Zealand at Lahore in 1955–56, Pakistan's first double century in Test cricket.

Ijaz Butt, eight Test appearances, and Abdul Kadir, four, were among those who followed Imtiaz. Both had their moments as batsmen. Butt scored a century before lunch against Kent at Canterbury in 1962, and Kadir made 95 (run out) in a Test against Australia in 1964–65. Then came Wasim Bari, who passed all previous wicket-keeping records for Pakistan and became the first Pakistani to complete 200 dismissals. He had his batting ups and downs, too, and came through as an obdurate rather than attractive batsman.

7

Technique and Concentration

THE TWO most important facets in the making of a good wicket-keeper are concentration and, as fundamental as it might sound, the ability to catch the ball. Nobody can ever hope to be a decent 'keeper if he simply cannot catch; although, of course, his ability to do this can be improved with good technique. Concentration is crucial because, in a Test match, a wicket-keeper can be behind the stumps for two days or more on the trot. It can be longer than a day in a county game and perhaps three hours or so in a club match. Whether taking a ball not hit by the batsman or catching a return from a fielder, the wicket-keeper handles the ball at some point in at least 75 per cent of the deliveries bowled in a match. Clearly, as the fulcrum of the fielding team, concentration is vital. An outfielder can wander a little bit, look up at the sky or chat with spectators to take a 'mental breather'; a wicket-keeper's concentration must not waver, and should be particularly intense from the moment the bowler begins his run-up.

It is more important for a wicket-keeper to watch the line of the ball than the length. So I would crouch with my left foot roughly on the line of the off stump at a distance from the stumps I thought appropriate to the speed of the bowler. Of course, if the batsman was left-handed, my right foot would be aligned close to the line of his off stump. This gave me a clear view of the ball leaving the bowler's hand. Sometimes if the angle of delivery changed – for example, with somebody bowling from round the wicket – I might stand a little wider, but never directly in line with the stumps.

As in so many sports, balance is important. When waiting for the ball to arrive, your weight should be evenly distributed on both feet, allowing you to move either way. The wicket-keeper does not normally know which course the ball is going to take when it leaves the bowler's hand, so he must be prepared to move in any direction. Often, of course, the bowler does not know, either!

Anticipation is an important part of keeping wicket – the ability to sense where the ball will end up. I remember when Jim Laker took his eight wickets for two runs in the Test trial at Bradford in 1950. Don Kenyon, the old Worcestershire opener, went back to a ball from Laker that turned and lifted. I could see Kenyon going to play a defensive shot, just placing the ball down on the legside. He played it from quite high, off the middle of the bat, and the ball brushed his pad as it dropped towards the turf. I dived and just got my left hand underneath the ball and held the catch. Don couldn't believe it. It was one of the best catches I've taken and a perfect illustration of anticipation.

It is vital for the wicket-keeper to get his body behind the ball. Nobody can be certain how the ball will behave once it hits the pitch – it could kick or shoot, move to off or leg – but the 'keeper has to stop it, even if he does not necessarily catch the ball. Not only does this prevent extras, it can also lead to a catch that might otherwise have been dropped. Virtually all regular wicket-keepers must, at some time and especially when standing up, have caught a batsman from an edge that has rebounded from, say, the 'keeper's chest or pads. If the stumper's body had not been behind the ball, a dismissal in this manner would not have been possible.

A certain amount of 'kidology' helps if a 'keeper does not catch the ball cleanly, but stops it with some part of his anatomy. Pick up the ball and throw it to a fielder or the bowler as quickly as possible. You will find that the spectators, some distance from the action, and even some of the fielders, might not realise the 'keeper had fumbled it.

So, once the wicket-keeper has got his feet in line, is well balanced, has anticipated, has his body behind the ball and is concentrating, what should he remember when it comes to actually catching the ball? Two main things: do not snatch the ball and always keep the fingers pointing outwards. Any 'keeper who snatches at the ball reduces his chances of catching it; the ball simply bounces out of the gloves. Do not move the hands forward to meet the ball, but wait and then 'give' with its momentum once it has arrived in the gloves. Do not snatch or flinch. Keep calm and watch the ball.

Wicket-keepers must never catch the ball like an alligator closes its mouth. The chances of dropping it vastly increase and, perhaps even worse, the risk of injury to the fingers goes up. You have to be only an inch or so awry in your judgement for the ball to hit you on the end of the finger. With the fingers pointing outwards – that is the same direction as the arms – a misjudgement will mean that the ball strikes you on the potentially less damaging area of the fingers on the inside of the hand. Pointing the fingers outwards also increases the gloved area and gives you more chance of catching the ball. More often than not, the ball arrives at around waist height. When this is the case, point the fingers downwards, towards the ground; if the ball is to either side, point the fingers away from the body. Catch high balls with the fingers pointing upwards.

The wicket-keeper is the focal point of the fielding side. He can make the fielding look better than it is and he can make it look worse. A 'keeper gathering the ball cleanly looks neat and it is his job to turn poor returns by fieldsmen into good ones. If the ball is dropping, say, ten yards short of the stumps, run to catch it on the full. Or, if it is not possible to make sufficient ground to catch the ball before it bounces, make sure you catch it with your gloves – do not stop it with your pads. Pass the ball to a fielder or bowler as quickly as possible so no time is wasted. The 'keeper should move up to the stumps whenever the batsman hits the ball. This allows the fielders to throw the ball in without the danger of overthrows. It also enables you to be in the correct position if a run out chance arises. Run outs can materialise from the most innocuous looking situations – perhaps the batsman slips or hesitates – and it is important that when this happens, the wicket-keeper is correctly positioned to take advantage.

A wicket-keeper knows better than anybody the speed at which the ball is coming off the pitch. In this respect, he can help his fellow close fielders by suggesting to the captain that they move back a yard, or come in a stride, depending on the pace of the pitch. A slip fielder standing too deep on a slow wicket will find the ball dropping a few feet in front of him; and one too close on a quick wicket will discover that the ball has shot past him before he has had time to react. The fielders will often realise they are standing in the wrong place only after it is too late; it is up to the wicket-keeper to suggest to the captain to tell them first.

Any captain worth his salt will consult his wicket-keeper. The man behind the stumps is perfectly positioned to judge whether the ball is moving in the air or off the pitch, seaming, swinging or spinning, keeping low or lifting; he can also tell how a particular team-mate is bowling. He could, perhaps, suggest a change of bowling, or an additional close fielder. No captain is obliged to act upon this advice, but he should seek it. If the captain does not ask the wicket-keeper's opinion, he is entitled to make his comments, anyway. A good skipper will not resent the intrusion.

A wicket-keeper can spread his enthusiasm throughout the entire team. A word of encouragement to a bowler or an acknowledgement of an accurate return from the boundary can do wonders for morale.

There was once an occasion in a Test match when Freddie Trueman had been bowling most of the day and looked totally exhausted as the last half-hour approached. Len Hutton, who was captaining England that day, came over to me and said: 'Do you think you could get Fred to stay on. I can see he wants a rest, but I'm keen to keep the runs down and I think he's the man to do it.'

'I'll certainly have a go, skipper,' I said. Walking over to Trueman, I asked him: 'How are you feeling, Fred?'

'Absolutely knackered,' he replied.

'Well, Fred, you might be knackered, but you're frightening the life out of that chap at the other end.'

'Frightening him? I couldn't knock a feather over.'

'Tell you what,' I said, 'on the fourth ball of the next over he's batting at that end, send down a bouncer at him. Bet it frightens him.'

'He's not frightened of me. I'm completely done.'

'Just bowl the bouncer, Fred, I'll be ready for it and we'll see what happens,' I said encouragingly.

Sure enough, the fourth ball of Fred's next over was a bouncer, but it was totally lacking in venom and presenting not the slightest physical threat to the batsman. There was certainly no fright in his eyes.

But a chorus of 'Well bowled, Fred!' echoed from the slips and short legs. I'd given them the word. Fred, looking somewhat surprised but clearly inspired by all these sudden compliments, went back and sent down a truly wicked bumper two balls later. This time the batsman was genuinely concerned. All the fielders clapped and I dashed up to him and said: 'Well bowled, Fred. You nearly got him and he's really scared of you.'

'Do you think it was that good?' he said. 'I'm going to have another couple of overs now and we'll get the bugger out.'

Obviously, all individuals are different. Trueman was the type of man who responded to encouragement and would continue to flog his body if he saw a chance. We kept the runs down that night, captured the remaining wickets the following morning and knocked off the runs to win the match.

I used to play three sports that helped my cricket. Hockey, a game in which great stamina is required, is particularly helpful for batting. A hockey stick is a similar shape to a cricket bat handle and the game involves the process of hitting a moving ball – the whole essence of batting. Speed off the mark is essential in hockey, as it is when attempting to scamper quick singles. Squash helped to improve balance and my ability to anticipate and move quickly to either side; it strengthened the leg muscles and thus increased 'springiness' and the distance and speed I could dive. Golf, which incorporated, in my case, 80 or 90 shots spread over three hours or more, exercised the mind and improved my concentration.

8

Equipment

A WICKET-KEEPER has the ball pounding into his gloves
every few seconds for hours on end. Sometimes, from fast
bowlers or rapid returns from fieldsmen, the 5½ ounce
spheroid of leather is travelling more quickly than the
national speed limit. He must crouch, jump, dive and run
in an open expanse of grass, totally unprotected from the
extremes of the elements – hot and cold, wind and sun. A
wicket-keeper should know how to protect himself. Bad,
ill-fitting clothes and equipment are a short cut to possible
temporary or permanent injury.

Damage to the body, especially the hands, is almost
inevitable to anyone who keeps wicket regularly. But it can
be minimised by good technique – principally keeping the
fingers pointing outwards – and the correct clothing and
equipment.

So what should a 'keeper wear? Starting from his feet:
boots (or shoes), socks, flannels, pads, jockstrap, box
(abdominal protector), shirt, sweater (if cold), inners,
gloves, cravat or knotted handkerchief (if hot), headgear (I
always wore a cap) and possibly a woollen pad to cover the
back, an accessory unknown to most of the cricketing
public.

Boots should be as light as possible. I will never forget the
first time I went to Australia. I had been to Northampton,
the home town of the boot and the shoe, to have a couple of
pairs specially made. One was studded and the other had
crepe soles and each pair was made from the best quality
leather. But they were far too heavy. In Australia, I noticed
all their players wore light-soled boots with the studs
incorporated, with the facility to insert additional rubber

71

studs if desired. The uppers, instead of being leather, were
of kangaroo hide, which was light and thin. Their pliability
gave the feeling that you could skip for a week without
suffering any soreness. I brought a couple of pairs back
with me and used them for years afterwards.

Nowadays, cricketing footwear is all much lighter than in
my time. It allows freer movement, although the modern
shoes do not hold the heels as well as the old-style boots.
But heel support is not essential for a wicket-keeper because there is no pressure on that part of his foot while he is
crouching to wait for the bowler to deliver. Even though the
boots worn by Ray Lindwall and Keith Miller were fairly
light, fast bowlers generally choose more substantial footwear as support and protection for their constantly-
pounding feet. Comfort, though, is probably the key word.

Socks, which should be made of wool, serve two main
purposes: they cushion the feet and absorb perspiration.
On a hot day, I might lose as much as five or six pounds in
weight and much of the perspiration would run down the
legs and into the boots. I would change my socks at every
interval. There is nothing less appealing than the prospect
of having to put on a pair of drenched socks for the final
session of play, so always remember to carry several spare
pairs. Some wicket-keepers wear more than one pair to
increase the cushioning effect and help soak up the moisture – especially on hard ground and hot days.

A wicket-keeper's flannels should have extra room
around the backside to allow the freedom of movement
necessary when bending down and up. There is nothing
more embarrassing than a split pair of whites. They can be
bought off the peg or, if you are a particularly awkward
shape, made to measure.

Batsmen are not the only people who must wear abdominal protectors. Some close-to-the-wicket fielders insert a
box and wicket-keepers must never go out unless wearing
one. One accident and your confidence could be ruined for
life, quite apart from anything else! Boxes, which used to be
metal, are now usually made from strong plastic and slip
comfortably into a pouch in the jockstrap. Make sure you
buy a cricket jockstrap – those for athletics, football and so

on often do not have the pouch. Boxes with straps attached and those with padding across the stomach for wicket-keepers used to be quite common; personally, I found both too cumbersome. Keep things as light as possible.

Wicket-keeping pads should be light and pliable, normally less bulky than batting pads. The modern trend is for pads that stop at the knee. That is fine for a wicket-keeper throwing himself about a long way from the stumps and attempting to stop balls from a fast bowler. The problems arise when, standing up to a bowler of Alec Bedser's type, the ball kicks to a greater height than you anticipate. There have been countless occasions when I have been grateful for protection above the knee.

I shall never forget playing for a local club in Canterbury, shortly after I joined the Kent staff. The captain announced: 'Well, Godfrey, you should have no trouble today. Our equipment is brand new. It's just come from the shop this morning.' But my heart sank when I saw this gleaming new equipment. The pads were designed for hockey goal-keepers – very tall and square and as stiff as boards. They dwarfed me and I could hardly move. The captain handed me the gloves and they were exactly the same – I could barely move my fingers.

So out I lumbered and, from the first ball of the match, the opening batsman struck an enormous straight six. 'Not bad,' I thought. 'This bloke's a bit useful. I'm not going to be required to take many balls behind the stumps. And thank goodness.' Unfortunately, from the second delivery the batsman attempted to repeat the shot. This time, however, the ball climbed to a great height, but almost vertically.

The captain yelled my name to catch it. I couldn't move, tripped and fell and the ball plummeted back to earth and landed about ten yards from my prostrate body. I felt such a fool. I asked the captain to excuse me for a moment, returned to the pavilion and put on the oldest pair of pads and gloves I could find. Suddenly, I could move my legs and fingers and ultimately had a reasonable match.

It is essential that a wicket-keeper's shirt fits properly. There should be plenty of room in the shoulders, to accommodate the moving arms and allowing a forward crouch without difficulty. But the shirt must fit neatly around the waistline as I discovered to my cost in a Test match against the West Indies at Lord's in 1950. 'Roley' Jenkins sent down a perfectly disguised and pitched googly to Clyde Walcott, who stepped down the track with the intention of hitting the ball over the pavilion. It turned sufficiently to beat the inside edge and bounced over the top of the stumps. But, as I jumped to gather the ball, my shirt came untucked from my trousers. My efforts to remove the bails were thwarted because gloves became entangled with shirt tail and Clyde was able to regain his ground. He finished 168 not out. Subsequently, I always wore a tightish shirt, similar to the T-shirts fashionable as casual dress nowadays.

I would wear a sweater only in particularly chilly conditions, and then, apart from in extreme cold, a short-sleeved one. A long-sleeved sweater restricts movement, and I found that I rarely became very cold keeping wicket. In hot weather, I wouldn't dream of wearing a sweater; it is all right for fast bowlers, who work up a sweat during an over and then run the risk of getting cold in between. It is essential that they keep their muscles warm. Although wicket-keepers keep warm during a day, there is a danger of even a slight breeze chilling the perspiration on your back. Many wicket-keepers suffer from back trouble and that is where the woollen pad comes in.

The idea was suggested to me while I was touring Australia for the first time in 1946–47. A dear old lady knitted me a square of wool with straps attached. I did these up at the front, and tucked it in my jockstrap at the back. It served me throughout my career. Wool has the property of absorbing some of the perspiration and not allowing the body to chill, even when a strong wind is blowing against the moisture. That is why mountaineers, and people working in cold and wet environments, often wear wool next to the skin.

People who keep wicket regularly should never wet inners. Use from day to day keeps them supple and plenty of moisture comes from the hands themselves. The club player, who keeps wicket only once a week, might consider it necessary to put his chamois leather inners under the tap because they are almost totally rigid. But the reason they are so stiff is simple: they were made wet by the chap who used them last week. The first thing I did with a new pair of inners was to put them on and bind each finger joint with Elastoplast. This provided greater protection to the joints – which receive quite a hammering in a career behind the stumps – and also allowed me to slip the outer glove on and off more easily, without removing the inner. Learn to protect your fingers early on in life.

When they arrive from the manufacturer, gloves are in no condition for use. It is important to make them supple. I would do this by placing them on the turf and pounding them repeatedly with a bat. Another procedure is to thump the fist into the centre of the opposite hand. This helps the fingers wrap around the ball more easily when catching it.

The sun and heat can become very fierce, especially on tour, so a cravat or handkerchief knotted at the front helps to avert the danger of sunstroke. It also prevents perspiration from running down the neck. Perhaps just once or twice during an entire career, you might feel a drop of perspiration around the neck. You could mistake it for a fly and it may distract you enough to drop a catch or miss a stumping. And that is a high price to pay.

I preferred a peaked cap to the floppy sunhat favoured these days by, among others, Bob Taylor and Alan Knott. The principal reason for headgear is to shield the eyes from bright sunlight, thus alleviating eye strain, and it seems to me that a cap offers more protection than the floppy variety. But again, it is no good wearing a peaked cap if you feel more comfortable in a 'floppy'. Comfort is essential.

Les Ames has told me that he used to put a slice of steak inside his gloves when keeping to Harold Larwood in the 'bodyline' series in Australia in 1932–33. Indeed, this was quite common practice in the days when wicket-keeping gloves provided scant protection. Personally, I never found it necessary. I remember once I got a painful bruise in the centre of my hand from not taking the ball cleanly. As a remedy, I worked a thin piece of plasticine into a circle, removed the centre (in the fashion of a large Polo mint) and placed it over the bruised area. This meant that, when I next caught the ball, the plasticine would take the impact, and not the bruise. If I suffered bruised finger joints, I would remove the Elastoplast from the outside of the inners and replace it with more substantial electrician's tape. I discovered that, by using electrician's tape in this way, I could continue with even a minor break and not suffer undue discomfort.

9

Bowlers I Would Have Loved to Have Kept To . . . But Never Did

FEW CAN have stronger credentials as the finest fast bowler of all time than *Dennis Lillee*. The great Australian announced his retirement from international cricket in January 1984, when, with 355 wickets, he was comfortably the most prolific bowler in Test history.

Anybody with a semblance of cricketing knowledge – and, I am sure, most people without – can appreciate Lillee's qualities: his sheer speed, his hostility, his dislike of batsmen, his cunning and his magnificent action. Yes, his action. Has there ever been a more fluent, textbook, perfectly-coordinated delivery stride?

Add to this potent armoury the crippling physical odds Lillee has had to overcome, and we have a truly remarkable sportsman. Lillee suffered a stress fracture of the vertebrae in 1973. Dennis was perhaps the only person who wholeheartedly believed he could make such a triumphant comeback. Looking back through newspaper cuttings, I have even discovered an article by Keith Miller, normally the ultimate optimist, under the headline: 'Forget Lillee – I cannot see him regaining peak fitness.' But Lillee himself refused to accept it. He punished his body back into shape, strengthened the muscles surrounding the spine, over-came the doubt – from other people, at least – and spasms of pain. By the winter of 1974–75, he was tearing into the England batting once again. Subsequent operations on his knees must have seemed almost inconsequential in com-parison with his back injury.

The spectator on the Hill at Sydney, in the pavilion at

Lord's or in the armchair in front of the television knows that Lillee has a rare talent. But to realise fully the extent of a cricketer's real greatness, one must play with or against him. And nobody has a better view of a bowler than the wicket-keeper. From crouching behind the stumps, I have been able to appreciate the control of Alec Bedser and the speed of Frank Tyson. I would have loved to have kept wicket to the bowling of Dennis Lillee.

Just how quick was he in those tearaway early days? Would I have been able to spot the difference between the ball that moved away off the pitch and the one that came back at the batsman? In his later years, when cunning and skill became Lillee's principal weapons rather than absolute pace, would I even have had the nerve to stand up to him? Quite possibly Lillee would not have wanted that – the sight of a 'keeper standing up to his bowling might have been an affront to his pride. I should think that the only fast bowlers in my time to rival Lillee's sustained brilliance for a decade or more have been Ray Lindwall and Fred Trueman. All three have been truly quick at times, used brain as well as brawn and had the commodity that stands the test of time – a marvellous action.

Mention of Lillee, of course, inevitably brings us to *Jeff Thomson*. Lillee and Thomson, Lindwall and Miller, Laurel and Hardy, Morecambe and Wise, bread and butter, gin and tonic. All the great double acts roll off the tongue. In the mid-seventies, Thomson was almost certainly faster than Lillee has ever been. In consecutive Australian seasons, 'Thommo' terrorised batsmen from both England and the West Indies. The threat he posed was not solely physical – he took 62 wickets in those two series.

Thommo propelled the ball from that remarkable slinging action. At the start of it, his right hand was just a couple of inches above the turf and I remember Barry Richards saying that, as the ball was hidden behind Thomson's body, the batsman had even less time to pick up the flight. Despite suffering from a glut of wides and no balls when he first came to England, Thomson was still a daunting prospect in this country. But it was on the fast Australian pitches, with their extra bounce, that he was at his most devastating. He could make the ball fly at the batsman's throat from little short of a length.

I wonder how far I would have had to stand from the stumps to gather the ball at a comfortable height. I can recall Thomson digging in a bouncer or two against England in 1974–75 which, after pitching, ballooned over Rod Marsh's outstretched arms and crashed second bounce into the sightscreen, perhaps almost 100 yards from the stumps. Frank Tyson, in Australia in 1954–55, was the fastest bowler I ever kept wicket to. If Thomson was quicker, then he was truly rapid.

Since I retired, perhaps only *Michael Holding* from the West Indies has rivalled Thomson for pace. Lillee, Andy Roberts, Colin Croft, Peter Pollock, Bob Willis, Wayne Daniel, Sylvester Clarke and John Snow are among other bowlers of extreme pace. But for me – and remember I did not keep to any of them – Holding and Thomson stand out.

Holding, though, was a different type of bowler from Thomson. Whereas Jeff's pace is generated largely from an explosive action, Michael's speed comes from a long, fluent run-up, allied to timing and suppleness of body. An outstanding quarter-miler as a young man, Holding glides across the grass and, after a long spell, has scarcely scuffed the bowling crease.

Holding's finest hour was at The Oval in 1976. On a slow, shirtfront of a pitch, on which Viv Richards and Dennis Amiss both made double centuries, Holding took 14 wickets – twelve of which were either bowled or lbw – a tribute to his accuracy and speed through the air. I would have loved to have kept to Holding – watching that distant figure moving deceptively quickly towards the stumps and, with apparently the minimum of effort, the release of a 100 mph bullet. And, when a wicket did fall, being part of the joyous West Indies celebrations would have been great fun.

Roberts, the non-smiler, is a highly intelligent fast bowler, likely to lull a batsman into false security with a 'slow' bouncer one ball and rip through his defences with a high-velocity one next up. Few bowlers have been able to bowl yorkers on demand more consistently than Roberts. I

79

wonder if I could coax a smile from that usually expression-less face?

Croft and *Joel Garner*, other members of the fearsome battery of fast bowlers to emerge from the Caribbean during the seventies, pose very individual problems for batsmen – and wicket-keepers. Croft uses the width of the crease more than any other of his contemporaries. Indeed, his left foot lands well outside the return crease when he is bowling from over the wicket – remember, if his back foot was to touch the return crease, he would be no-balled. The different angle means that balls pitching, say, 18 inches outside the off stump are not necessarily safe to leave alone.

Garner, 6 ft 8 in tall, can extract lift from even the most placid pitch. He releases the ball from a height of more than eight feet and, especially if he pitches just short of a length, is virtually impossible to score from. Consequently, Garner is the world's most effective bowler in one-day cricket. Although not as quick as Holding, Roberts and Co., Garner might have forced me to stand as far back to handle his steepling bounce.

Fast bowlers have been the trend in the two decades since I retired from the first-class game. And, although Australia and the West Indies have been more endowed with these speed merchants than other countries, England have un-earthed a couple of outstanding ones. *John Snow*, with that lovely easy action, won the series virtually single-handed for Ray Illingworth's side Down Under in 1970–71. The Aussies simply could not believe it when Snow was omitted from the England touring team of 1974–75. You could always tell when Snowy's tail was up – he rolled his sleeves still higher up his arm. I would have enjoyed being behind the stumps and watching an English fast bowler hurry batsmen from all over the world into error. Snow did that in his prime.

Bob Willis, like Lillee, is another who has confounded his critics. Bob's knee problems, although not as serious as Dennis's back injury, threatened to end his career more than once. But Willis continued coming back, captained England and became, after Trueman, only the second Englishman to take 300 Test wickets, finally overhauling

Fred's record of 307 in the first Test of the 1983–84 series in New Zealand. Bob, although having a natural in-swinger's action, can hustle the ball away from the right-hander. For years, he has been England's only reliable fast bowler. Willis, whose admiration for Bob Dylan was such that he added the name of the American singer-songwriter to his, has often provided the lone hostility in the England team; his triumph has been one of dedication, determination – and skill.

Mike Hendrick and *Geoff Arnold* are bowlers who played for England after my time and, although not in the really fast category, would have been interesting to keep to. Hendrick's international career has been somewhat frustrating. His accuracy is almost uncanny and his action textbook yet, in 30 Test matches before becoming a South African 'rebel' and being banned from playing for England for three years, never took five wickets in a Test innings. That is a disappointing statistic for a bowler of Mike's ability. I believe the reason he has not been more successful at the highest level is that he does not pitch the ball far enough up. He has always been difficult to get away and, by giving the ball greater length, and allowing it extra time to move, he would prompt more errors. A good way to tempt a bowler to pitch up more is for the wicket-keeper to stand up to the stumps – which is what I would have done when keeping to Hendrick. I am convinced Mike would take more wickets if he asked the 'keeper to stand up. Arnold was one of the most effective new-ball bowlers in the seventies and, in overcast or humid conditions, could swing the ball alarmingly.

Each of the three other major Test-playing nations has produced one outstanding opening bowler in recent years – and I would have enjoyed keeping to them all. *Imran Khan* of Pakistan has been described as the 'fastest bowler on the county circuit' by more than one batsman I have spoken to. Before a stress fracture of the shin interrupted his career during 1983 – he was unable to bowl a ball during the Prudential Cup – Imran had just about reached his peak. He had perfected a booming inswinger which, delivered faster than most cars can travel, is sometimes almost unplayable. A magnificent athlete – and strikingly handsome to boot – Imran in full flight is an inspiration. If he ever doubts that he will be able to recapture his effectiveness after injury, Imran should pick up the telephone and give Dennis Lillee a call.

Richard Hadlee showed in the 1983 series against England that a fast bowler does not need a run-up stretching most of the way towards the boundary to generate pace. Some – like Holding – do, but not all of them. Hadlee cut his run by more than half from his earlier days and yet, with little apparent effort, he can rush the best batsmen into their shots. It is all a case of coordination. Hadlee has taken more Test wickets than any other New Zealander.

India, not a country renowned for quick bowlers, have certainly found a top-quality one in *Kapil Dev*. Although not quite in the very highest bracket when it comes to speed, Kapil can still make the best of them jump around. His greatest weapon is the away-cutter, which will move either very late in the air or off the pitch – or both. Kapil's captaincy of India in their 1983 Prudential Cup triumph was an inspiration.

Imran, Hadlee and Kapil, apart from being exceptional new-ball bowlers, are also talented batsmen. Along with *Ian Botham*, a bowler who is prepared to try anything for a wicket even if it means conceding extra runs, and *Mike Procter*, a square-on fast bowler and, when he injured his knee, useful off-spinner, they are the finest all-rounders of their generation.

An altogether different challenge is posed when keeping wicket to spin bowling. To fast bowlers, the stumper stands maybe a pitch length from the stumps, feels the ball thudding into his gloves and must throw himself in all directions in an effort to catch or stop the ball. Spin bowlers, or medium-pacers to whom a 'keeper stands up, demand nimble footwork, fast hands, sharp eyes and plenty of self-confidence. I believe that standing up provides a more thorough examination of a wicket-keeper's ability than standing back.

And there have been plenty of slow bowlers I would have enjoyed 'keeping to. No single country has produced more since my retirement than India, whose great quartet of *Bishen Bedi, Bhagwat Chandresekhar, Srini Venkataraghavan* and *Erapalli Prasanna* mesmerised and strangled the confidence and attacking scope of so many opponents.

Bedi, with his multi-coloured puktas, was a left-armer who relied more on subtleties and variations of flight than extracting enormous turn from the wicket. A batsman might mis-read the trajectory of the ball and play too early or be deceived by a quicker one. Bedi and Derek Underwood were rivals as the best left-arm spinner in the world for a long time. Bedi finished his Test career with 266 wickets from 67 Tests; Underwood so far has 289 from 79.

Venkat and Prasanna were off-spinners in the classical mould, but perhaps the most interesting of the four to keep to would have been Chandra. His bowling arm was withered by a boyhood bout of polio, yet, curiously, this disability helped make him the great bowler he was. He could twist and turn his arm unusually and 'whip' it through at a deceptive pace – indeed, he has been known to bowl a bouncer. Chandra was primarily a wrist spinner, but occasionally cut the ball and could move it both ways off the pitch. I have often wondered whether I could tell which way the ball would spin upon pitching. That would have been one of the great fascinations when keeping to Chandra. Perhaps more than any other cricketer, Chandra's story is a fairytale. The Indian boy who catches the wretched and often crippling disease of polio, spends months in hospital, is encouraged to lead a normal life and then actually uses that disability – the thinness and flexibility of his right arm acted like a whipcord – as the fundamental aspect of his success.

I have kept wicket to *Underwood*, although not as often as I would have liked and never on a rain-affected pitch. That would have been an education: watching the most deadly bowler on a helpful track running through the opposition. Other spinners who would surely have provided me with fascination include *Ashley Mallett, Phil Edmonds* and *John Emburey*. But of current Test slow bowlers, one stands out: *Abdul Qadir* of Pakistan, of course. He has proved that an almost extinct breed – the leg-spinner – can operate successfully in modern Test cricket. The England batsmen in 1982 were palpably unable to spot his top-spinners and googlies from his orthodox leg-break. From my position behind the stumps, I bet I could have done. Abdul's greatest asset is that the batsmen of the eighties are simply not used to facing bowlers of his type. It would have been laughable to think that, 30 years ago, a batsman would be in the England side without ever having batted against a decent 'leggie'. That is to take nothing away from Qadir, though. He would have taken wickets even in the days when batsmen were familiar with his type.

During my career, I played against most of the world's leading bowlers. From the vantage point of batting just 22 yards away, I was able to assess their particular qualities. And I can tell you there were times when I would rather have been studying them from that other excellent viewing position – behind the stumps.

Ray Lindwall and *Keith Miller*, for example, would have been an altogether more comfortable proposition if I had been keeping wicket to them, instead of batting against them. Lindwall possessed the lot – pace, movement and super action, while Miller, exceptionally quick when the mood took him, was the master of the unexpected.

Neil Adcock and *Peter Heine* from South Africa were top-quality fast bowlers. Although our Test careers just over-lapped, I never played against *Wes Hall*, the tall, gangling fast bowler – and another with a classical action – from the West Indies. I kept wicket to Wes just once – in a game in Bombay to celebrate the centenary of Indian cricket which raised around £1 million for charity.

Although I did not play against Hall for England, I was in opposition to two other legendary bowlers from the West Indies. *Sonny Ramadhin* and *Alf Valentine*, whose mystifying spin bowling confused batsmen and inspired a song, certainly caused England many problems.

The problem with Ramadhin was that batsmen simply could not tell which way the ball would turn. That he usually bowled in his cap, his sleeves buttoned at the wrist, merely added to the aura of mystery. He bowled orthodox off-spinners and leg-breaks, but he could also make the ball move away from the right-hander without delivering it from out of the back of the hand. Valentine, left-arm spinner, was a more traditional type of slow bowler, although his skill was sharply honed. He picked up 33 wickets in four Tests in England in 1950, when barely in his twenties.

Clyde Walcott went into the nets for two solid days at the start of the 1950 tour with the sole purpose of getting accustomed to Ramadhin. Clyde tells me that, after that 48-hour session, he could predict with some certainty which way the ball would turn when it pitched. Walcott, remember, was an outstanding batsman with a superb eye. If it took him that long to 'spot' Sonny, imagine the problems our batsmen encountered on facing Sonny just a handful of times throughout the summer. I wonder whether I could have spotted the vagaries of spin from behind the stumps.

Lance Gibbs was a magnificent, but orthodox off-spinner who, until Dennis Lillee passed his figure, was the highest wicket-taker in Test history. Lance's control was impeccable. *Garry Sobers*, whom I played against many times, was, of course, the complete cricketer. He could bowl the lot: fast, medium-pace, orthodox left-arm and googlies and chinamen.

Other fine bowlers of my time, to whose bowling I never kept wicket, include the admirable *Fazal Mahmood*, perhaps Pakistan's finest new-ball bowler until Imran arrived on the scene; *Alan Davidson* and *Graham McKenzie*, whose Test debut came after I finished my international career, those two fine quick bowlers from Australia; and, of course, the South African spinner, *Hughie Tayfield*, off whom Johnny Waite captured so many stumpings, and leg-spinner *Richie Benaud*. The list is almost endless. But it is safe to say that I would have preferred keeping wicket to most of my contemporaries than batting against them. Not only because I would have remained out in the middle longer, but also to satisfy my natural curiosity.

I have seen all the great bowlers of the last fifty years, either in direct opposition or as a spectator. As I say, I know the particular qualities of those I played with and against

better than those I merely watched either before or after my
first-class career.

Some of the game's greatest bowlers were dead before I
was born; others had retired before my awareness of cricket
grew. Of all the bowlers before my time, I think one stands
out as a bowler I would dearly have loved to have kept
wicket to. *Sydney Barnes*, believed by many to be the finest
of them all, sounds in many ways a similar bowler to Alec
Bedser. A bounding approach to the wicket was followed
by a ball delivered at around medium-pace, liable to move
either way off the pitch. Barnes had long, strong fingers
which he wrapped around the ball and, from what I have
read and heard about the man, was absolutely devastating
at times. I would certainly have stood up to him.

I wonder how the likes of *F. R. Spofforth*, the Australian,
and *Charles Kortright* of Essex, allegedly the fastest bowler in
the world for a time, would have compared with Tyson and
Trueman. I kept to Bill Voce, but never *Harold Larwood*. Les
Ames often speaks about Larwood's extreme pace, developed from the small frame of a man standing only about
5 ft 7 in in height. On the 'bodyline' tour of 1932–33, could
he have been as fast as Tyson in Australia in 1954–55?

Wilfred Rhodes, the only man to take more than 4,000
first-class wickets, was an outstanding all-round cricketer.
He opened the batting for England – and he also went in at
number eleven. I wonder if he would have been such a
prolific wicket-taker in a more recent era and how he might
have compared with left-arm spinners of my time such as
Tony Lock and Johnny Wardle. How about *George Hirst*,
that other wonderful Yorkshire all-rounder who completed
the unique 'double' of 2,000 runs and 200 wickets in 1906?
And, of course, what sort of cricketer, what sort of man was
W. G. Grace? He took 2,876 wickets during his first-class
career, so he cannot have been a bad bowler, even if some of
those wickets were claimed by asserting his authority and
personality over both batsmen and umpires. In these days
of the 'personality cult' Grace would clearly have been a
major figure. But I doubt whether one man could now be so
singularly dominant in a sport.

Colin Blythe, the famous Kent bowler before the First

World War, captured 2,506 wickets in a career from 1899 to 1914. 'Charlie' Blythe, who was also a keen violinist (the grace and rhythm of his bowling was almost musical), was a legendary figure in the history of the county around the turn of the century.

Blythe was a left-arm spinner who was never below third in the national bowling averages from 1909 to 1914 and headed them in the last three of those years. He captured 100 wickets at 18.63 in Test cricket. He died in action in France and there is a memorial in his name on the county ground at Canterbury. Blythe, along with Derek Underwood and *'Tich' Freeman*, was probably the best slow bowler in Kent's history. I kept to Tich just once, in a charity game on Bearsted Green in 1938. His record was extraordinary. He took 304 wickets in 1928, 298 in 1933 and, in eight seasons between 1928 and 1935, dismissed 2,090 batsmen. He played in just twelve Test matches and it was said he was not a great bowler against great batsmen. But I know Don Bradman had a high regard for him. Freeman was little more than five feet tall, but could turn the ball sharply from leg and also possessed the googly and effective top-spinner.

The list is enormous, bowlers I would have loved to have kept to . . . but never did.

Left: Syed Kirmani, the excellent Indian wicket-keeper, in ballet pose. *Adrian Murrell/Allsport Photographic*

Below: Alan Knott in action during the last of his 95 England appearances before his three-year Test ban for his involvement with the 'rebel' tour of South Africa. Knott is at full stretch attempting to stop a leg glance by Allan Border off Ian Botham against Australia at The Oval in 1981. Mike Brearley is at slip.
Adrian Murrell/Allsport Photographic

Alec Bedser was a magnificent bowler to whom I usually stood up to the stumps. Alec is pictured bowling for Surrey against MCC in 1951. *S & G Press Agency Ltd*

Three generations of the Parks cricketing family. Jim was the finest wicket-keeper batsman I have seen, apart from Les Ames. Jim senior completed the unique 'double' of 3,000 runs and 100 wickets in 1937, and Bobby is currently a fine prospect with Hampshire. *Allsport Photographic*

Syed Kirmani proudly clutches his trophy and bottle after being voted the Gordon's Gin Wicket-keeper of the World Cup following India's triumph in 1983. *Bill Smith FRPS*

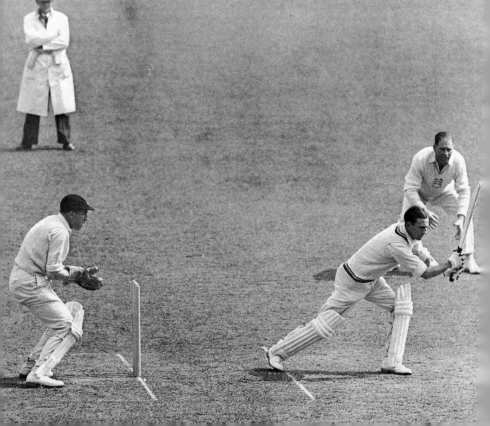

Top left: I was delighted to accept Gordon's Gin's offer to be chairman of their wicket-keeping awards. Here I present David East with the 1983 annual award. Keith Fletcher, the Essex captain on the right, was the first to acknowledge that East's performance behind the stumps was an important factor in Essex's County Championship triumph. *S & G Press Agency Ltd*

Bottom left: Len Hutton, one of the finest of all batsmen, drives through the offside while playing for Yorkshire against MCC in 1948. George Dawkes of Derbyshire is the wicket-keeper and Essex's Tom Pearce the fielder. *S & G Press Agency Ltd*

Below: 'Fiery' Fred Trueman has been the central figure in more cricket stories than just about any other player. He was not a bad bowler, either, with a wonderful action and follow-through. *S & G Press Agency Ltd*

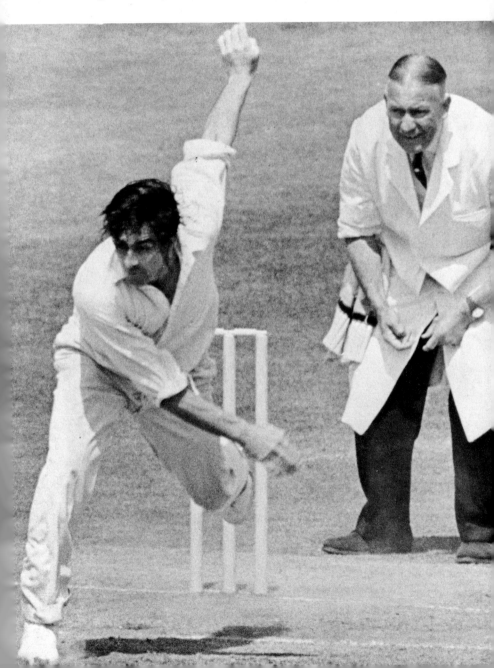

I never kept wicket to faster bowling than that delivered by Frank Tyson during the 1954-55 series in Australia. Here Frank is bowling for MCC against the West Indies in 1957. *S & G Press Agency Ltd*

Above: Jim Laker, the finest off-spinner I have seen, during his finest hour. Jim took an unprecedented 19 wickets for 90 in this match, the Old Trafford Test of 1956 against Australia.
S & G Press Agency Ltd

Right: Keith Miller, a dynamic all-rounder and master of the unexpected, after releasing one of his high-velocity deliveries. I would have liked to have kept wicket to Keith; unfortunately, my experiences of receiving his bowling were restricted to having a bat in my hands!
S & G Press Agency Ltd

Above: Dennis Lillee, who retired from Test cricket with a record 355 wickets, appeals with typical enthusiasm and traps Graham Gooch leg before during the Old Trafford Test in 1981. Lillee's comeback from a horrifying back injury was one of the cricketing fairytales of the seventies.

Adrian Murrell/Allsport Photographic

Left: Batsman's view of West Indies fast bowler Michael Holding.

Adrian Murrell/Allsport Photographic

10

A Conversation with Les Ames

Godfrey Evans I was twelve years old when you went with the England team on the 'bodyline' tour to Australia in 1932–33. I remember it causing quite a rumpus at the time, but was probably too young to appreciate the full implications. But putting the political storm aside, I've often wondered just how quick Harold Larwood, Bill Voce and 'Gubby' Allen were. As the wicket-keeper, you were in the best position to judge . . . apart, that is, from the unfortunate Australian batsmen.

Leslie Ames Harold and Bill were desperately quick, and Gubby was only a yard or two behind. The three of them played only rarely together, so comparisons are not easy. I've always felt that Larwood and Voce should have played more with each other for England – remember, Bill was never selected for a Test match in England – but, of course, Maurice Tate was in his prime at the time.

G.E. How would you compare Larwood and Voce with two bowlers of my time – Trueman and Statham?

L.A. Different eras, circumstances, batsmen, pitches and so on make comparisons almost impossible. But I would say that Trueman and Statham were more consistent and bowled better as a pair.

G.E. You mentioned Maurice Tate. How similar do you think he was to Alec Bedser?

L.A. For three or four years, Maurice was magnificent. His accuracy allowed me to stand up to him. His stock delivery was the one that pitched on middle or middle and off and moved away towards the slips; this made standing up fairly straightforward because I got a clear view of the ball from the moment it left his hand. He hardly ever put

89

one down the legside. I think he was a little quicker than Bedser and this was accentuated because he had the ability to make the ball gather pace off the pitch. Once Maurice lost that little bit of 'nip', he was not the same bowler.

G.E.   Alec was often difficult to stand up to, because I would lose sight of his inswinger as the ball went across the batsman's body. Alec became a truly great bowler when he introduced the leg cutter into his repertoire.

L.A.   For those three or four years, when Maurice was at his peak, he was the better bowler. But over the course of their entire careers, Alec gets my vote. Maurice did not have to contend with the lbw law that was subsequently introduced. So, in his day, the ball moving away from the right-hander was far more beneficial.

G.E.   That's right. When Alec started his career, the lbw law meant that a batsman could be dismissed by a ball pitching outside the off stump. As a result, virtually every medium-pacer in the country developed the inswinger. I think Reg Perks and Fred Root, both of Worcestershire, were the first genuinely fast bowlers to bowl inswingers. This really tucked batsmen up, not allowing them the freedom to hit through the offside.

I shall never forget Alec bowling in the first of the two Melbourne Tests against Australia in 1950–51. The pitch was green and the atmosphere humid. Alec was moving it all over the place. It was interesting, although extremely difficult, to keep to him. And I was delighted to let through only four byes in the Australian innings of 194. It could have been 24 in the morning session alone. Nevertheless, we got only one wicket on that first morning.

L.A.   The only bowler I've seen with the ability to move the ball away towards the slips in the way Maurice Tate could was Ian Botham. But Ian is not as accurate as Maurice by any means. He bowls far too many short-pitched deliveries and he's not quick enough to prevent batsmen getting into position and hitting him square. Maurice – like Alec to a certain extent – was a container of batsmen, whereas Botham can be quite expensive. When Maurice's rhythm was right, he hardly ever bowled a loose ball.

G.E. How about two of the great Kent spin bowlers you saw – 'Tich' Freeman and Doug Wright?
L.A. They were both leg-spinners. But that's where the similarity ended. Tich gave the ball a lot of air; he often deceived batsmen, who would advance from their crease in an effort to smother the spin. But they discovered the dipping delivery pitched farther down the wicket than they anticipated. They were stranded. The turning ball would beat the outside edge. I got so many stumpings off Tich's bowling in that way.

Tich was a much better bowler than he was often given credit for. He was not a great spinner of the ball, but was very accurate for a leggie. He often didn't seem to bowl well against the really great batsmen – perhaps it was a mental problem and the reason he didn't play for England more often than he did. Somehow, the selectors usually preferred Walter Robins or Freddie Brown.

I remember playing for Kent against Gloucestershire in front of 20,000 spectators at Bristol. They had come to see Wally Hammond, who had returned from his triumphant tour of Australia in 1928–29. As Wally was walking out to bat, Tich said to me: 'I'm going to toss the first ball up a little bit more than usual. Sometimes Wally drags his foot, doesn't he?'

'Okay, Tich,' I replied.

Freeman, who had a habit of hitching up his trousers and shrugging his shoulders before each ball, threw this one right up in the air. Wally misjudged the length slightly and went to drive. He missed the ball, dragged his foot and I stumped him first ball. You could have heard a pin drop as Wally walked back to the pavilion. It was like when we got Bradman out first ball – he was bowled by Bill Bowes – in his first Test of the 'bodyline' series. There was stunned silence.

I often think Freeman's looks went against him. He never looked much of an athlete. He was a little, balding man who appeared older than he was, and neither a brilliant batsman nor fielder. Robins and Brown were both better batsmen than Tich.

Occasionally, Tich would bowl a little short, because he'd

be trying to spin it too much. He also had a very good top spinner that was difficult to pick. The batsmen would play for the leg-spinner, but the ball would gather pace off the pitch and be through them before they could re-adjust. Tich also had the googly, but that was not so well disguised.

G.E. I know exactly what you mean about Freeman not looking the part. The Australian wicket-keeper in the fifties, Gil Langley, suffered from the same problem. He was overweight, his shirt tail always hanging out and he never looked tidy. Often, the Aussie selectors seemed to choose another 'keeper simply because he was better turned out. Langley was superb. He hardly missed a thing and I saw him take some breathtaking catches off inside edges standing up. Keith Miller thinks he was one of the best 'keepers he's seen.

Okay, Les. I know you've said it's difficult to compare players from different eras, but how about some thoughts on Hedley Verity and Derek Underwood? You've played with and against Verity and, of course, seen plenty of Underwood through your Kent connections.

L.A. Hedley was accurate and turned the ball quite considerably. But on good pitches, he didn't present too much of a problem to batsmen. Derek, though, is even more accurate. Even on the best pitches, he takes some getting away, although he doesn't spin the ball as much as Verity did. Underwood is more of a cutter. And, of course, if Derek gets a pitch that helps him, he's virtually unplayable. The greatest batting line-up of all time wouldn't last long against him. Not Jack Hobbs, not Don Bradman, not anybody. Verity was only truly effective on real sticky wickets, and good batsmen didn't have much trouble with him most of the time. I think Derek is the slightly better bowler.

G.E. But didn't Verity once get fifteen wickets in a Test match at Lord's? Would Underwood have got that many?

L.A. I think Derek would have got even more in that match. Certainly, with him in the side, England would still have won by an innings. If Derek had played in my time, I think he would have gone down as one of the greatest bowlers of all time. The wickets weren't covered then. Often we played with a little moisture in the grass and in those conditions Derek is unplayable. But he gets so few really helpful pitches these days with the covers going on as soon as it starts to rain. Yet he still takes a hundred wickets almost every season.

A lot of people reckon Underwood should try to flight the ball a little more and bowl slower. I think that is entirely wrong. His main ball is the one pushed through, with the slower one as a variation. Most left-armers' stock delivery is tossed up, with variety coming from the quicker one.

G.E. When Jim Laker got his nineteen wickets at Old Trafford in 1956, he was giving the ball plenty of air. The batsmen were going down the track and not getting to the pitch of it. They then made a half-hearted shot and were being caught at, say, short leg.

L.A. Sounds just like Tich Freeman.

G.E. Let's talk a bit about batting. You were always renowned as a marvellous runner between the wickets. Who was the best runner you batted with?

L.A. No doubt about it, Godfrey. Arthur Fagg. We had such a great understanding. Arthur was a good judge of a run and I reckon I wasn't bad, either, and often we didn't even need to call. A bit like Herbert Sutcliffe and Jack Hobbs when they played for England. There was no need for a call every time, they just went. If there was ever any doubt, either Arthur or myself would say 'No' in a sharp, definite way. The secret of good running is not to hesitate. If you run immediately or say 'No' straight away, you'll be okay.

Wally Hammond was a good runner, although he often seemed to pinch a single off the fifth or sixth ball of an over. When he was playing well, he would certainly count the number of deliveries and hog the strike. If you weren't careful, you'd be batting with Wally and hardly face a ball. But I think all the great batsmen are pretty good counters. Len Hutton was the same, although I think he, unlike Wally, would make sure he didn't have much of the strike when the quick bowlers were making it fly about. Not because he was scared, just that he thought there was more chance of being dismissed.

G.E. It has always been a mystery to me why Denis Compton was such a bad runner. He was a genius as a batsman, such a beautiful timer of the ball and a brilliant all-round athlete. But he just couldn't judge a run, would hesitate a lot and get into a right muddle with his calling.

You played with that great Kent left-hander, Frank Woolley. Have you seen any other left-hander to approach his ability?

L.A. Graeme Pollock from South Africa comes as close to Frank as you could possibly get. Frank was the greatest English left-hander of all time. And he wasn't a bad bowler, either. I remember one year he broke his finger during Canterbury week in August and he didn't play again that season. Up to then, he had scored more than 2,000 runs and taken 163 wickets. He also had a superbly safe pair of hands. He held more than 1,000 catches – a world record. Only Jack Hobbs scored more runs. Frank's motto was: 'Hit the ball hard, high and as often as possible.' If there was nobody out in the deep, Frank would try to hit the ball there. He didn't worry if it was in the air or not. He hated being tied down. Pollock is exactly the same. He likes to hit the ball in the air into the open spaces. It is a great shame we haven't seen more of him in Test cricket.

G.E. What's your feeling about the England players who went to South Africa and were banned from Test cricket for three years?

L.A. I've always been a great believer in playing cricket anywhere in the world. I know the players were warned of the possible consequences, but I think they were entitled to go. And a three-year ban does seem a severe punishment. In an ideal world, politics wouldn't interfere with sport. But it does seem amazing that we have a situation where South African-born and West Indies-born cricketers are playing alongside each other in the England team, while a number of our best players have been banned because they went to South Africa.

But when I talk about South Africa I always think of that 'timeless' Test at Durban in 1938–39. It was the longest match of all time and finished with my Kent captain Brian Valentine and myself batting. We needed 696 to win and the game finished with us on 654 for five because we had to go to Cape Town to catch the boat home. A telegram was sent to see whether the boat could wait while the match was completed. But it couldn't. So the match was left as a draw, just as it looked as though we would pull off an amazing win. The pitch was as good at the end of the match as it had been at the start ten days earlier. The reason was that a little light rain which fell every evening between three-thirty and four o'clock helped bind the pitch together. It rolled out flat each morning.

G.E. Who was the finest wicket-keeper from abroad during your time?

L.A. There was a fellow from South Africa called Horace Cameron. He died at an early age from a virus infection shortly after the 1935 tour to England. Many people thought he would have become one of the greatest of all wicket-keepers. He was also a fine batsman. During the 1935 tour, Cameron hit 30 (444666) in one over off Hedley Verity in the match against Yorkshire. Arthur Wood, the Yorkshire wicket-keeper who was always fond of a joke, shouted down the wicket: 'Hedley, you're all right now. You've got him in two minds. He doesn't know whether to hit you for six or four!'

I always thought Bertie Oldfield was a magnificent 'keeper. So graceful and stylish – and I didn't see him miss much. But Don Bradman told me many years later that Bertie missed quite a few little nicks that nobody knew about. Don Tallon had the edge, though, and I was amazed he was not selected for the Australians' 1938 tour.

G.E. What did you think of Paul Gibb?

L.A. Paul wasn't a great 'keeper. But he had superb concentration and was a keep-fit fanatic. He went for a run every morning and always seemed to be playing squash. He made his name more for his batting. He could really stick around. He did very well when he came back to play for Essex after he had retired from Yorkshire.

G.E. Paul went to Australia as the number one 'keeper for the 1946–47 series. But in the first Test he had a bit of a nightmare. He dropped both Bradman and Hassett, who made a century apiece, and Australia totalled more than 600. I took his place in the side after that. Of course, Wally

Hammond was the England captain on that tour. How good was Wally?

L.A. Possibly the best all-round cricketer England has produced. He had a marvellous cover drive and could hit very hard indeed off the back foot. He often used to step away to make room for himself and hammer the ball through the offside. He had such a wonderful eye. He eliminated the hook because he considered it a dangerous shot. And, of course, he was a top-class bowler. He got 80-odd wickets in Test cricket, bowling at about the same pace as Alec Bedser. He certainly could move it around a bit. But, because of his tremendous batting, he didn't bowl as much as he might have done. He was also a magnificent fielder. He could field at short leg or slip, and never seemed to dirty his trousers, he picked up the ball so cleanly and quickly.

G.E. Wally gave me a lot of help and encouragement when I first started keeping wicket for England. I know he was considered selfish in some aspects of life. For example, he always travelled by car – and not on the team coach – in Australia in 1946–47. But I don't think that's something to be ashamed of. For years, the amateurs changed in different dressing-rooms and stayed at different hotels from the professionals.

11

Cricket's Chatterboxes

Do NOT let anyone kid you that cricketers, who can spend hours on end batting, bowling, fielding and keeping wicket, behave as though they are in a public library. Silence is most certainly not the order of the day. Some of the best players could out-natter Hilda Ogden. Occasionally, the words may be barbed, but generally the mood is jovial. Comments in the field are rarely more pointed than what might be termed legitimate gamesmanship.

One of the best talkers was the former Somerset and England opener Harold Gimblett, who earned an indelible place in cricket folklore with a lightning century on his debut against Essex at Frome in 1935. Harold's chatter was amazing: sometimes he would still be talking when the ball was on its way from the bowler's hand.

There was one occasion when Harold was batting at Bath, a delightful ground surrounded by hills, on a turning wicket against Doug Wright.

'The ball's turning. There will be a few wickets going down today,' I said to Harold from behind the stumps.

'Yes, Godfrey, there certainly will be. There is only one thing to do if the ball is pitched up,' replied Harold. By now Doug had reached the stumps and, as he released the ball, Harold finished his sentence, 'and that's hit it.'

Harold took a pace down the pitch, judged the length to perfection, and struck the ball straight over the sightscreen. You could not wish to see a more sweetly timed six. However, it did not always work out like that for Harold.

Kent were playing Somerset at Maidstone and again Wright was bowling to Gimblett. Harold claimed he could easily pick Doug's googly. We all knew that it was virtually impossible to distinguish between Wright's superbly-disguised variations. But Harold would have none of it. As each ball came down, he was saying 'Leggie', 'Googly', 'Leggie', and so on. Suddenly Doug let his quick one go – a yorker just outside the leg stump. Harold, realising he had got this one wrong, shouted 'Ouch!' just before the ball landed on his toe. He jumped up and down in pain for a couple of minutes and all the Kent lads were trying their best to hide their laughter. Harold, seeing the joke, turned and said: 'Doug did me then all right, Godders. I think I'd better keep quiet from now on while he is bowling.'

Two of the great talkers in the Kent side were Brian Valentine, our captain, and Les Ames. They were usually in the slips or gully and golf was a common topic of conversation – how well they were putting, how long they were off the tee, or whether they were hooking or slicing. Perhaps their chats rubbed off on me, because I quickly became a keen golfer. When the game became quiet from my point of view – no wickets falling or the ball not coming through to me very often – I would often start talking to the batsmen. Where was he staying? What was the hotel like? Things with no association with the game at all. Of course, some batsmen were known not to like the chat – which meant I had them at a slight disadvantage. It disturbed their concentration. There was no malice in my actions – just a little bit of gamesmanship.

I remember Dickie Dodds, the old Essex opening batsman, was smashing the Kent bowling all round the ground. I mentioned that he was in line for the fastest century of the season, for which he would win a prize of £100, and that he should continue hammering away. He tried one big hit too many and was dismissed just short of three figures. Colin Ingleby-Mackenzie once rushed to within a few runs of a century against us at Southampton before he, too, fell for the quickest century chatter. I cannot exactly recall what he said on getting out. But it sounded something like: 'Basket!'

Fred Trueman, of course, was one of the most renowned talkers in the history of the game, and the reputation was not gained for nothing. If a batsman played a straight bat to one of Fred's best deliveries, he would glare down the pitch. His comments were uttered in what might be described as a loud whisper. There was a time when Fred was tearing in to bowl when the batsman walked away from the wicket. The umpire stretched out his arm and Fred, almost into his delivery stride, was forced to pull up.

'Stupid sod,' he said. Then, quick as a flash, he added: 'Sorry, umpire. I don't mean you. I'm talking about the silly chap who was walking in front of the sightscreen.' Nobody really believed Fred, however.

I was batting with Denis Compton in the Adelaide Test of 1946–47. Denis – and also Arthur Morris in the same match – scored a century in each innings and I took 95 minutes to get off the mark in that second innings, having been bowled first ball by a Ray Lindwall swinging full toss in the first innings. When Denis had the strike, all the fielders were on the boundary, but they clustered around me when I was facing.

Denis said to Don Bradman, the Australian captain: 'This is not cricket, Don.'

'We want Godfrey to face the bowling – it is the only way we can win the match,' replied The Don.

You would be surprised what we can see from the middle. Comments along these lines are frequent: 'Look at that lovely girl sitting on the grass just to the left of the sightscreen,' or 'What about the beauty next to the President's tent and wearing the large hat?' Most spectators, of course, are unaware of this aspect of the game. They cannot hear all the chatter from the boundary.

Freddie Titmus and Peter Parfitt, those Middlesex and England players, were a pair of real chatterboxes. Parfitt would often be heard to say: 'Come on, Titters, give it a bit more air,' or 'Push one through a bit quicker, Fred.' There was one occasion when I was batting with Colin Cowdrey at Lord's. Colin was playing in subdued vein, quite content to push the ball back to the bowler. Parfitt was saying: 'Give it some air, Titters,' while Titmus's line of conversation to Cowdrey was: 'Come on, Kipper, give it a go.'

Fred thought that batsmen attempting to attack his bowling would be more likely to make errors. So Fred flighted the next delivery more in the hope that Cowdrey might be tempted into an indiscretion. It did not quite work. Cowdrey quickly picked up the length and direction of the ball and hit it over long on for six. As the ball soared over the boundary, I heard Fred say: 'Why pick on me, Colin? I haven't done you any harm.'

Yorkshiremen, with their dry sense of humour and penchant for cutting one-liners, do as much on-field talking as anybody. Most of their words are exhausted by moaning and quarrelling amongst themselves and I have more than once seen their former captain, Norman Yardley, place himself on the boundary to escape from the bickering between some of the Yorkshire players. On occasions Johnny Wardle, seeing Fred Trueman totally shattered towards the end of a long, hard day, bowled his over in less than two minutes before Fred scarcely had time to catch his breath. Fred would say: 'Johnny, for Pete's sake slow down a bit. I need a breather. And I've got a date tonight. At this rate I'll never make it.'

Brian Close was a great talker, too. He would get at any player he thought was not pulling his weight. I often felt there was more to it than just talking to members of his own side, more an attempt to sap the batsman's concentration. 'Closey' was not alone, though, in employing crosstalk between the slips, short legs or gully in an effort to distract the batsman. Many counties and Test sides did it, and still do. If Closey, who always seemed to field on top of the batsman with his determined jaw jutting, led the chorus from the close fielders, there was certainly no shortage of chat coming from the bowlers. A typical Fred Trueman comment to a batsman who had edged a lucky four might be: 'If you fell in a pile of manure, you'd come up smelling of roses.'

There is one Yorkshireman whose concentration must be particularly difficult to distract. Geoff Boycott is a man whose desire and resolve to make large scores requires a devotion to duty that necessitates his pushing everything else from his mind. I must say I have always found Geoff most interesting to talk to. He has never been anything than courteous to me, so I find it difficult to understand his reputation for controversy. I do accept, however, that he sometimes bats in a selfish manner, playing more for himself than the side. But many of the great players have had the same approach and never received the same criticism as Geoff.

Most of the counties had their incessant talkers. I have already mentioned Harold Gimblett, but Somerset had another man who liked a good natter. Bill Andrews, a pacy inswing bowler, was once bowling a succession of balls down the legside to me. I was swinging the bat at every one, but seldom made contact. Finally, Bill shouted down the pitch at me: 'Godders, you're an old woman. You couldn't knock the skin off a rice pudding.'

Ellis Robinson, a Yorkshireman who played for Somerset, said to me when I hit two of his off-spinners into the pavilion at Taunton during one of my rare centuries: 'Hey, Godfrey, do you want to get me t'sack?'

Derbyshire had Cliff Gladwin, known as the 'Gaffer' because he always seemed to be in charge, and Alan Revill was also a keen talker. Cliff was bowling well one day, I got a thick edge, and as the ball went over the top of Alan's outstretched hand at slip he turned to me and said: 'Get one a bit nearer, Godfrey, and I'll have you.'

In the following over, I attempted a similarly ambitious shot, but this time got a thinner edge and Alan took a brilliant diving catch with his right hand just inches off the ground. I looked round and Alan, with a broad grin on his face, said: 'I told you so, Godfrey. You didn't believe me, did you?'

Vic Jackson, an Australian who played for Leicestershire, could talk. I well remember Jack Walsh, another Aussie, confusing Paddy Corrall, the Leicestershire wicket-keeper at the time, with his prodigiously-spinning chinamen and googlies. Paddy often did not know which way to go. But Jackson could spot the variations and would say to Paddy as each ball was coming down: 'Googly, chinaman, chinaman, googly,' and so on. It might have helped Paddy, but more than anything Vic's talking put off the batsman.

Northamptonshire also had a couple of Aussies who talked a lot – Jock Livingstone and George Tribe, who bowled in a fashion similar to Jack Walsh, although perhaps a little more accurately. When Jock was batting, he and I carried on an almost continuous conversation. I was trying to sap his concentration and he, in his turn, hoping I might miss a chance if one came my way. On one occasion at Northampton, Jock got the better of things and made a magnificent double century. As he passed 200, I said: 'Well played, Jock.' He replied: 'Thanks, Godders. I'm feeling fine apart from a dry throat after being out here talking to you for so long.'

George Cox, the Sussex opening batsman, was a lovely character. Many was the time he turned to me after mistiming an attacking shot and having to run two instead of collecting a boundary and said: 'Damn it, Godfrey, if I do this too often, I'll be tired before I get my century.'

George was a brilliant cover point. I would hit the ball to where he was fielding, move as if to run and see George glaring at me, saying: 'Don't you dare, Godfrey.' I called his bluff once at Hastings and nearly paid the penalty – his throw was half an inch off target, with me in full flight, but still a yard short. I never did it again.

Three of Hampshire's greatest chatterboxes were Colin Ingleby-Mackenzie, their captain, medium-pace bowler Vic Cannings and Leo Harrison, the county's wicket-keeper. I am sure Colin's talking – his enthusiasm, repartee and encouragement – was a major factor in Hampshire's winning the County Championship in 1961. When a catch went down, there was Colin saying: 'Don't worry, old boy, there's always tomorrow. We'll murder them.' Vic Cannings's approach was slightly different. If somebody dropped a catch off his bowling, Vic, who later coached at Eton, would say: 'What's up, mate? Were you thinking of your wife's sister?' Leo Harrison's barrage of banter from behind the stumps – especially when he felt the opposition were playing for a draw – made Hampshire one of the liveliest sides to play against.

Leslie Todd was not always the most popular player in the Kent side with other counties. Once at Northampton, Leslie had made a century in the first innings and I knew he dearly wanted to get one in the second as well – a feat he had not previously achieved. He had scored about 78 second time around and looked certain to realise his ambition. I could hear mutterings of discontent from the fielders about his hogging the crease, when we should have been pushing the score along to make a declaration. I attempted a drive but, by the time I discovered the ball was not quite up to me, I had committed myself. I skied it to deep mid-off. I always held out hope that a fielder might drop the catch, so I started to run. 'Toddy', thinking the catch would be swallowed and knowing it was the last ball of the over, stood his ground. The fielder did drop it and, as I was halfway down the pitch, I yelled to Toddy: 'Come on.' I was running to the danger end – or so I thought – but the Northants player, seeing Todd so late in starting, picked up the ball and flung it to the end where Toddy was running, hitting the stumps with Les still a yard or two short. The air was blue and Todd muttered all the way back to the pavilion. The Northants players, though, gathered round, thanked me, roared with laughter and said: 'Serves him bloody well right! He should think of the team – not himself.'

Reg Simpson, of Nottinghamshire and England, was one of the finest players of fast bowling in history. He was once asked whether he was scared of being hit by the ball and replied: 'If a heavyweight boxer can avoid a left hook from two yards, sure I must be able to get out of the way of a ball from 22 yards.' Not a bad theory and one, I'm sure, Ted Dexter had in mind when batting against the fastest bowlers. A pity that I could not always apply it. Once when I asked Keith Miller after he had bowled me in Melbourne 'What did I do wrong?' He simply replied, with a wry smile: 'I was just too quick for you, Godders,' and planted an imaginary punch on the end of my chin.

Above: Johnny Waite, an excellent wicket-keeper batsman, is the only man to have played in 50 Test matches for South Africa. Here he loses his cap in an effort to gather the ball during the Headingley Test of 1955. Brian Statham is batting.
S & G Press Agency Ltd

Left: Alan Knott, with his passion for physical fitness, has lost none of his agility and skill over the years. Graham Johnson, his Kent colleague, watches as Knotty plunges to his right during the 1983 NatWest Trophy Final against Somerset. The ball is nestling safely in his right glove. *Adrian Murrell/Allsport Photographic*

The bails are off and Rodney Marsh lets out another raucous appeal. On this occasion Mike Brearley survived. *Adrian Murrell/Allsport Photographic*

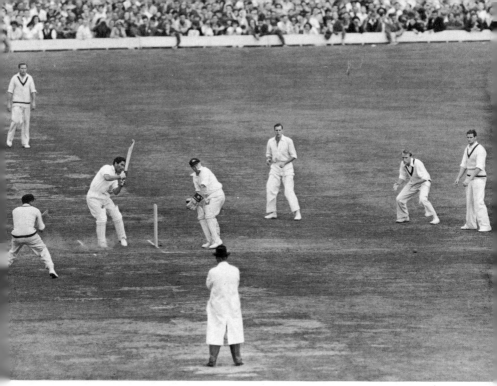

Denis Compton makes the winning hit at The Oval to complete England's recapture of the Ashes in 1953. The fielders are: Alan Davison (short leg), Ray Lindwall (point), Gil Langley (wicket-keeper), Ron Archer (gully), Graeme Hole (second slip) and Keith Miller (first slip).
The Photo Source

This dive was during the third Test match against the West Indies at Trent Bridge in 1950. People often said that I was never reluctant to throw myself about! *The Press Association Ltd*

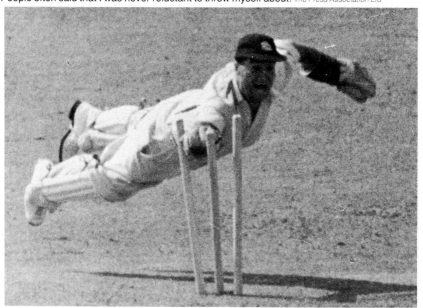

Top left: In the presence of a genius. I've gone wide for this one, but the Don hammers the ball square on the offside during the 1948 series. Bill Edrich is at slip. *The Photo Source*

Bottom left: My motto was always: 'Go for everything.' Sometimes it meant hurling myself through the air. Here I attempt to stop a return from Len Hutton during the Adelaide Test in the 1950-51 series. Bill Johnston is the Australian batsman making his ground. *The Photo Source*

Right: I square cut during an innings of 66 against India at Headingley in 1952. Madhav Mantri is the wicket-keeper. *S & G Press Agency Ltd*

Below: John Murray, normally the personification of elegance, dives full-length in an attempt to gather a wild return during the Lord's Test against India in 1967. Ajit Wadekar is the batsman. *S & G Press Agency Ltd*

Above: Bertie Oldfield, the Australian, was one of the 'keepers I admired as a boy. He is pictured here behind the stumps as Wally Hammond unleashes his famous cover drive. *Marylebone Cricket Club*

Upper left: 'Old Jack' Blackham, the great Australian wicket-keeper of the last century, who played in 35 Test matches. *Marylebone Cricket Club*

Centre left: J.J. Kelly, Blackham's successor, who represented Australia on 36 occasions. *Marylebone Cricket Club*

Bottom left: Herbert Strudwick, for years the most prolific wicket-keeper in history and a man whose hands, without the benefit of modern-day protection, took a terrible battering. *Marylebone Cricket Club*

Right: My team that would play in the imaginary match of my dreams: Len Hutton, Barry Richards, Don Bradman, Wally Hammond, Denis Compton, Neil Harvey, Garry Sobers, Godfrey Evans, Ray Lindwall, Jim Laker, Fred Trueman, Michael Holding (12th man). *The Press Association Ltd*

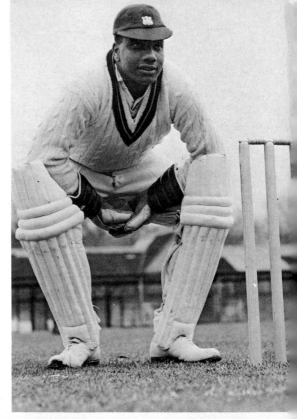

Right: Clyde Walcott, an excellent wicket-keeper with a safe pair of hands and huge reach, quite apart from being a destructive batsman, at the start of the 1950 West Indies tour to England.

S & G Press Agency Ltd

Below: Alan Knott, Les Ames and myself, three Kent and England wicket-keepers spanning half a century, share a joke with John Murray. Cricket, both on and off the field, has always been great fun.

12

Questions and Answers

THROUGHOUT MY playing career and subsequently, I have been asked many questions about cricket. By people who are lovers of the game, by budding wicket-keepers or those who are already highly competent behind the stumps, by young men who want to make a career in the game, by people – perhaps ladies – whose cricketing enjoyment comes from admiring the trees round the boundary. In fact, just about every type of person has quizzed me on cricket.

I could fill an entire book, let alone a single chapter, with all the questions – and answers I have given. Here, though, are samples of the type of question I am regularly asked. Remember, the answers are mine. Not all cricketers will share the same views.

Question: What made you want to become a wicket-keeper?
Answer: As a schoolboy, my idol was Leslie Ames. I wanted to imitate him, be like him in every way. Les was a wicket-keeper, so that is what I wanted to be.

Q: Would you not have preferred to be a bowler, batsman or all-rounder?
A: Once I fully appreciated Les Ames's role in the game – and, therefore, my role as well – it struck me that wicket-keeping is a rewarding position to fill. The man behind the stumps is involved in the game non-stop, more than any other player in the team. I realised I had the dual benefit of imitating my hero and also having the best job in the side. Wicket-keepers are often proud of their bowling – for some reason they normally seem to bowl leg-breaks – but they usually get little chance to demonstrate it beyond the confines of the nets. Probably just as well!

Q: Are good wicket-keepers born or can they be taught?
A: Most of the top wicket-keeper's talent comes from natural ability. But there is no reason why a good fielder – or batsman or bowler for that matter – cannot successfully take up wicket-keeping. Obviously, the later the switch is made, the more difficult it becomes. Jim Parks, who played for England as a batsman before he donned the gloves in earnest, and Alan Knott, who joined Kent's staff as an off-spinner could also bat a bit, are examples of men who successfully transformed.

Q: What makes a good wicket-keeper?
A: Perhaps the most important thing is that the person must *want* to be a wicket-keeper. *Want* to be involved all the time. *Want* to sweat in the heat. *Want* to take the occasional physical battering. Once he has decided he is prepared to do this, then things like technique come into it. Catching the ball is essential – both on the full or half-volley, which require very different techniques. He should not snatch at the ball, should wear the correct equipment. Always be prepared to encourage fielders and bowlers – even if he himself is feeling a bit dejected. Pass on advice to the captain – the wicket-keeper can often see things that nobody else spots. The wicket-keeper is never inactive, but if he wants constant involvement he is sure to enjoy himself.

Q: How do current 'keepers compare with those from your era? Have techniques changed?
A: The main difference is that, in my day, the wicket-keeper stood up to the stumps whenever possible. To my mind, standing up gave the bowler something to aim at, usually making him pitch up the ball more and committing the batsman to a stroke. As a result of the 'keeper lurking just behind him, the batsman is very cautious when playing forward for fear of lifting his back foot.

Of course there is the other side to the argument. Modern-day 'keepers will claim that standing back means they drop fewer catches and concede fewer extras. Today the ball is a different texture from my day – the shine lasts longer and it does not get so soggy and soft in wet conditions. Consequently, it stays newer and swings for a longer period – another reason for standing back.

I always maintain that if a 'keeper has the ability and the self-belief he should stand up to the stumps whenever possible. Some catches might go down, but he will compensate by making the occasional stumping. His close presence, too, will be an additional distraction to the batsman. Standing up also eliminates the run to the stumps each ball to gather the return from a fielder. In some cases, the fact that the 'keeper is already at the stumps will lead to a run out. Don't forget the thrill provided to the crowd by a legside stumping or a run out when the batsman is not quick enough on a sharp single.

As I say, there are pros and cons on both sides. But, if a 'keeper is standing up and the going gets tough, he must not allow his pride to rule his head. He should drop back to where it is more comfortable.

Q: Do you think cricket has changed for the better?
A: Generally, yes. The outstanding difference is in the quality of fielding. It is magnificent now compared with my day. The players are fitter, perhaps largely because of the demands of one-day cricket. The money earned – especially by the top players – is very good. Yet there are certain aspects I am not so keen on. The impregnated leather used to make cricket balls means the shine lasts longer, which has encouraged the fast bowlers and, disappointingly, a type of medium-pacer whose main aim, it seems, is to keep the runs down. The spinner – and especially the leggie – has been almost killed off. They are at a disadvantage on two counts: the shiny ball is more difficult to grip – hence spinners' accuracy declines – and the desire for containment means captains are often reluctant to employ a slow bowler.

Another thing I dislike with modern cricket is that teams tend to set out not to lose, rather than to win. I would have thought – and I'm sure the spectators paying for entertainment would feel the same – that it should be a case of try your damnedest to win and, if that becomes impossible, then settle for a draw. Perhaps the pressures provided by

107

money, television, sponsorship and the media mass cover-age have caused this negative approach.

Q: Do you think there are any characters in the game today?
A: Yes, but not as many as a few years ago. It's much harder to be a character. But I doubt if anyone will tell Ian Botham when to go to bed. The character does what he wants – has a good time and perhaps breaks a few rules or treads on a few people's toes along the way. But few of these extrovert cricketers allow their enjoyment of life to affect their per-formance on the field.

Q: Do you think the selectors have chosen the right wicket-keeper in recent years?
A: For a decade and a half, Alan Knott and Bob Taylor have dominated the England scene and there cannot be much arguing with that. Occasionally, the selectors have chosen an inferior wicket-keeper for one-day matches, but the plan has not been a success.

One thing I feel very strongly about, though, is that two wicket-keepers should always go on an England tour no matter how few matches are played by the one not picked for the Test matches. For example, Bob Taylor was the lone specialist stumper on the tour to Fiji, New Zealand and Pakistan in 1983–84. The selectors must have been mad! I know it saved money, but that is taking economy to ex-tremes. If the selectors had chosen a decent deputy to Bob – and there were a number about – they would have been looking to the future. After all, Bob was 42. Graeme Fowler, the Lancashire opening batsman, was the man to step in in an emergency and Paul Downton was in South Africa, ready to join the England team if anything hap-pened to Bob. But joining a tour midway through is never satisfactory. Perhaps the most damaging aspect of selecting only one wicket-keeper for a tour is that it must make all the other young 'keepers in the country think there is only one spot available. Their chances of getting into the England set-up are reduced by half. What could be more discourag-ing?

Personally, I was disgusted with the selection committee for the 1983–84 tour and I'm sure John Murray – who was a selector chosen to advise on the wicket-keepers before he resigned because the rest of the committee took no notice of him – felt the same. A prospective successor to Bob should have gone on the trip – and money no object. The wicket-keeper is one of the most important men on the field, so the two best available must always be with any touring team.

Q: Would you have liked to play one-day cricket?
A: I would have loved it. If I am batting, I like to score runs quickly. My motto has always been that you have a bat to score runs with – even though I still hold the world record for slow scoring in Test cricket, 95 minutes before scoring my first run. That was done for a special reason, to save the Test match, and it also allowed my partner Denis Compton to complete his second century. One-day cricket is here to stay. People should make the most of it and not make excuses about the difficulties of playing three- or five-day cricket one week and a limited-over game the next. What could be better for the spectator than getting runs, wickets *and* a result all on the same day?

Q: How were you able to dominate the wicket-keeping scene for so long?
A: There is always a certain amount of luck attached to success and I certainly had my share. One of the most important reasons was that, when I joined the Kent staff, the county had two of the outstanding 'keepers in the country on their books. Watching Les Ames and 'Hopper' Levett – who would have played more than once for England if he had played for another county – taught me a lot. They were always willing to pass on advice and encouragement. I loved the game, so it was no hardship spending many hours at the county ground learning and improving my trade. Once I started to play for England, there were three main reasons for the success I was fortunate to enjoy – a certain amount of talent (natural and learnt), my sheer enjoyment of it all and my durable physique.

Q: Do records play an important part in a cricketer's approach?
A: Some cricketers live for records. To others, they do not

make the slightest difference. In retrospect, I suppose some cricketers look back and think what they might have achieved in the pages of *Wisden* by being just a little more careful or bolder at times. Many cricketers don't even know it when they break a record. For instance, Denis Compton knew that, by scoring his seventeenth century in 1947, he beat Jack Hobbs's record. But when he made 300 in three hours against N.E. Transvaal at Benoni in South Africa, on the 1948–49 tour, he had no idea it was the quickest triple century of all time. Incidentally, Denis kept trying to get out after he reached each milestone – 100, 150, 200, 250 – and he finally achieved it when he got to 300. I would have been the only Englishman to score a century before lunch in a Test match at Lord's against India in 1952 if I had got just a couple more runs in the morning session. As it was, I was just glad to be not out at lunch.

Q: How well were you paid in your day – compared with modern cricketers?
A: The extraordinary change in players' wages was caused by the Kerry Packer revolution. There is no doubt that cricketers were underpaid compared with other sports – but whether it has gone too far only time will tell. I must say that, even though cricketers in my time were underpaid, the money would still buy a lot. My salary was £500 a year, until my last two years when I received £600. And some expenses were paid by the county. The pay when I made my Test debut in 1946 was £25, not bad in those days. But I suppose I'd sooner earn £2,000 today. A top-class player – that is one who plays for England – might be able to earn between £40,000 and £70,000 or even more per annum. In our day, anything over £1,000 was good. One could happily retire after ten years or so nowadays, but that would have been impossible a few years ago.

Q: What were your most memorable dismissals?
A: I suppose my first catch in county cricket stands out – against Derbyshire at Gravesend in 1939. Not so much for its brilliance, but because it was my first. Other dismissals I will never forget include catching Sid Barnes off Jim Laker at Trent Bridge in 1948; picking up Neil Harvey down the

legside off Frank Tyson at Melbourne in the 1954–55 series; Alan Davidson off Brian Statham at Sydney in the same rubber; catching Sam Loxton off Freddie Brown at Brisbane in 1946–47; stumping Jimmy Burke off Laker at Lord's in 1956, and many more. My finest catch, though, was probably one I held at Scarborough. The Players had declared, leaving the Gentlemen a hefty target on a good pitch. Billy Sutcliffe opened the innings for the Gentlemen and Alec Bedser was bowling. Alec sent down one of his 'boomerang' deliveries, a big inswinger, and Billy moved down the pitch to try to hit the ball with the swing over mid-on's head. I was trying to judge the swing and realised that, if Billy did not hit it, I must dive full-length to my left to stop it. I did this, and although Billy made contact, the ball was not deflected much off its line. I landed at full stretch and, to my astonishment, the ball smacked right in the centre of my left palm and stayed there.

Q: What are your outstanding cricketing memories?
A: There are thousands. Literally thousands. Being part of the England team that won the Ashes in 1953 was an enormous thrill. So was beating South Africa by two wickets off the final ball of the first Test in 1948–49. My 98 before lunch against India at Lord's in 1952, a century for England against Ramadhin and Valentine at Old Trafford in 1950, taking those 95 minutes to get off the mark at Adelaide in 1946–47, thus allowing Denis Compton to complete his second century of the match.

Other memories include a quick 47 in 'Laker's Match' at Old Trafford in 1956, when I was stumped by Len Maddocks, while almost shaking hands with Ian Johnson, the bowler; scoring 74 against South Africa at Trent Bridge in 1947, when an England rearguard prevented defeat; being selected for Kent as a batsman in 1939; my Test debut in 1946; hitting the first six by an Englishman on the New Wanderers Ground off Neil Adcock; running six with Brian Close off the bowling of Trevor Bailey at Lord's without the aid of overthrows; hitting the winning run to secure the Ashes in Adelaide in 1954–55; and Doug Wright taking a hat-trick watched by the Duke of Edinburgh at Canterbury.

I suppose I also remember incidents with a touch of humour attached, as when Denis Compton was bitten by a dog when trying to carry it off the field (although I'm not sure Denis laughed too much!) and Freddie Brown trying to persuade Compton, Trevor Bailey and myself to go to bed at midnight on New Year's Eve at the Kelvin Grove Club in Cape Town. The next day I scored 60-odd and we won the match.

Q: Have you any memories of important misses?
A: I should say so. I missed the chance of stumping Gerry Gomez in Barbados off the bowling of Jack Ikin. I caught the ball and returned it to the bowler so quickly that I didn't realise Gerry was out of his ground. I was so taken aback that I missed the next ball – which proved that a 'keeper should forget whatever happened from the previous delivery. Leeds in 1948 was probably my worst nightmare match – when Australia scored more than 400 on the final day to win. Jim Laker twice lured Don Bradman out of his ground, but each time I missed the ball and the stumping chances went begging. In the same game, Denis Comptom bowled a full toss to Arthur Morris – he missed it and so did I, with Arthur comfortably out of his ground.

Then there was Neil Harvey at Old Trafford. I was standing back to Trevor Bailey when Neil slashed at the ball. It hit me on the chest and bounced away. Neil was four at the time and went on to score 122. I understand John Arlott kept saying things in his broadcast such as: 'Neil Harvey is now 57 – if only Godfrey had caught him when he was four.'

13

The Kent Connection

ONE OF my proudest achievements is to have extended Kent's tradition for outstanding wicket-keepers. From James Aylward, the first Kent 'keeper of note in the eighteenth century, to Alan Knott, no other county has produced so many fine performers behind the stumps.

A measure of the quality of Kent's wicket-keepers over the years can be gained from the fact that the county has had four players who have each taken more than 1,000 first-class dismissals – F. H. Huish, Leslie Ames, myself and Alan Knott.

But let us take a quick journey back to the days when cricket was in its infancy, and when wicket-keepers had no protection for their hands – they did not even wear gloves. As a result, many of the old players' hands were sickeningly contorted by countless broken bones. Jem Mace, the famous prize fighter of the last century, is known to have told Ted Pooley of Surrey and Middlesex that he would rather 'stand up to any man in England for an hour' than take his place behind the stumps for five minutes.

One of the most famous early cricket paintings is by Francis Hayman and entitled 'Cricket at the Artillery Ground'. The wicket-keeper is believed to have been William Hogarth, a friend of Hayman's, and he has no protection at all in the picture – neither pads nor gloves. Wicket-keepers in those days were treated just like the other fielders.

Kent wicket-keepers were making their mark more than 200 years ago. Around 1744, in a match between Kent and England at the Artillery Ground, a man called Kips from Eltham completed the first stumping when he removed

Bryan. This game, which Kent won by one wicket, was the first great match from which the full score has been preserved.

The two best-known 'keepers in the second half of the eighteenth century were probably William Yalden of Surrey and Tom Sueter, who played for the Hambledon club after matches for both Surrey and England. Sueter was probably the first man to develop some of the basic techniques of wicket-keeping still used today.

James Aylward, who played for Kent from 1779 to 1793, scored more than 1,000 runs for the county with his left-handed batting. Aylward was still an active and fit man late in life and played in a match at Lord's in 1802, when 61 years of age. Then came the man who truly established the Kent tradition for great wicket-keepers.

Edward Gower 'Ned' Wenman, one of seven of his family who played for Kent in the nineteenth century, took 47 catches and completed 33 stumpings during a county career that began in 1825 and extended until 1854.

Round arm bowling brought the need for protection, and wicket-keeping pads and gloves were displayed at the Great Exhibition in 1851; soon afterwards, they became commonplace. Thomas Box, who played for Sussex from 1832 to 1856, was one of the great early padded stumpers and was immortalised in a comment by William Lillywhite: 'Have me to bowl, Box to keep wicket and Pilch to bat and then you'll see cricket.'

After Box and Surrey's Thomas Lockyer, a pioneer at taking balls on the leg side, there were four outstanding professional wicket-keepers who developed the art towards the twentieth century. Mordecai Sherwin of Nottinghamshire, who once stood for Parliament; Richard Pilling, from Bedfordshire, who played for Lancashire and was the first man to stand up to the stumps regularly; Ted Pooley, who represented both Surrey and Middlesex; and George Pinder, who kept wicket to the legendary George Emmett.

The top amateurs of this period were the Hon. Alfred Lyttleton of Middlesex, who ultimately became Colonial Secretary and is related to the modern jazz trumpeter, Humphrey Lyttleton, and E. F. S. Tylecote, who became the first Kent wicket-keeper to play for England. Tylecote, also an outstanding batsman, once scored 404 not out for Classical v. Modern while at Clifton and caught five and stumped two in the Gentleman v. Players match at The Oval in 1876. Tylecote's most famous innings was probably the 100 not out he scored against the Australians at Canterbury in 1882. The attack included Palmer, Garrett, Boyle and Giffen.

John McCarthy ('Old Jack') Blackham, the Australian widely regarded as the first of the great modern wicket-keepers, toured England eight times. Between 1877 and 1894 he played in 35 Test matches against England, catching 36 and stumping 24. He normally stood up to the stumps, although sometimes the pace of Spofforth forced him back. Blackham was succeeded by J. J. Kelly, whose record was 39 catches and 16 stumpings in 33 Tests against England.

England's answers to Blackham and Kelly were Gregor MacGregor, who played Rugby football for Scotland, and captained Middlesex when they won the Championship in 1903, and 'Dick' Lilley of Warwickshire, who learned much from Blackham, and was probably England's best wicket-keeper before the First World War.

Kent, though, had not ceased producing fine stumpers. Edward Henty played 117 matches for the county between 1865 and 1881 and became the first man to pass 200 dismissals for Kent. He became a first-class umpire when his playing days were over. John Pentecost had 124 victims in 65 matches between 1882 and 1890, but failing eyesight brought his career to a premature end. The amateur Manley Colchester (1880–1895) claimed 165 victims. Then came Frederick Henry Huish, a dapper man who, between 1895 and 1914, accounted for 1,328 batsmen, and is still fourth on the all-time list behind Bob Taylor, John Murray and Herbert Strudwick – Knott, though, could soon overtake him. Jack Hubble followed Huish and dismissed ten Gloucestershire batsmen at Cheltenham in 1923. George Wood, who was in Archie Maclaren's side that beat the 1921 Australians at Eastbourne, played for Cambridge either side of the First World War and then represented Kent, for whom he scored

2,773 runs and helped in the dismissals of 131 batsmen. He played in three Test matches for England against South Africa in 1924.

Elsewhere, Strudwick, a neat and unobtrusive 'keeper, was England's first-choice for a long time, George Brown of Hampshire played seven Test matches, and George Duckworth was the regular before Leslie Ames, my schoolboy idol, took over. For Australia, 'Bertie' Oldfield, one of the greatest of all wicket-keepers, succeeded Hanson 'Sammy' Carter, and Horace Cameron is considered by many as South Africa's best 'keeper. He died at the age of 30 shortly after South Africa's tour of England in 1935.

It is with Kent, though, that we are principally concerned. The county was fortunate in that, when Ames, who dismissed 121 batsmen in 1928 and a world record 127 in 1929, was away on Test duty, they had a 'keeper of the quality of William Howard Vincent Levett to step into the breach.

'Hopper' Levett, whose enthusiasm was infectious, helped me a great deal in my early days. 'Godfrey, look at your feet,' he said to me dozens of times. 'You cannot reach the wicket in that position. What's the good of being where you are if you cannot stump the batsman when he moves out of his ground?' I'm convinced his coaching and advice helped my advancement. I remember Hopper, who toured India with MCC in 1933–34 and played in one Test, telling me what happened when, playing for the Gentlemen against the Players at Lord's, he attempted to catch a mighty skier from Big Jim Smith. Hopper shouted: 'It's mine.' As the ball continued to gather height and then plummeted downwards, Hopper started running round in circles in an effort to get underneath it. He eventually fell flat on his face and the ball dropped a couple of yards away. 'Don't rush madly for skiers, take your time and sum up where to place yourself,' he would often tell me.

With two such magnificent 'keepers as Ames and Levett on the Kent staff, I thought I might have to wait a long time for my chance. But in 1939 Ames was out of the side with a bad back and Kent were concerned about the resultant decrease in batting strength. As I had been scoring a few runs in the Second XI, I was selected as a batsman. I remember well my first innings, against Surrey at Blackheath, and being caught by Laurie Fishlock on the legside boundary after hooking an Alf Gover bouncer. I scored eight.

However, I did keep wicket before the War when Hopper, a Territorial, joined the Army. Ames decided to retire from wicket-keeping after the War, even though he retained his place as a batsman, so I immediately became Kent's regular 'keeper. I was selected to play for England in that first season after the War and made my debut against India in the third Test at The Oval in 1946.

Kent again possessed excellent 'keepers to take my place while I was playing for England. Derek Ufton, an England soccer international who played for Charlton, was a gifted all-round sportsman who eventually gave up wicket-keeping to concentrate on his batting. This was when George Downton, the father of Paul (who started with Kent and now plays for Middlesex), played for Kent. Maurice Fenner, an ex-RAF Squadron Leader who captained the Combined Forces side and later became Kent secretary, and Tony Catt, a powerful man, also played.

Then came a small, dark-haired man with a passion for fitness and flexibility. He joined the Kent staff as an off-spinner, who could also bat a bit and keep wicket. Alan Knott, a man who always rose to the big occasion or crisis, averaged 32.75 in his 95 Test matches for England. He might yet play Test cricket again and he has propelled the tradition of Kent, the county of the 'keeper, into the space age.

14

Wicket-keeping Awards

IMAGINE MY delight when, in early 1982, I was asked by Roy Mantle of Counsel Ltd, the advertising agency acting for Gordon's Gin, to be chairman of the Gordon's Gin Wicket-keeping Awards. I would head a panel, selecting monthly winners and picking an annual Wicket-keeper of The Season. This was a particular honour for me. Awards for batsmen, bowlers and even fielders have been handed out for many years. But, until Gordon's stepped in, the poor old stumper had never been recognised.

My first duty was to select a panel. I decided I wanted two more wicket-keepers, a captain, fast bowler, spin bowler, and representative from the media. My first thought for one of the other wicket-keeping positions was John Murray. 'JT' was the world dismissal record holder for a number of years until Bob Taylor exceeded his figure. John has a keen awareness of the contemporary game and, particularly, the current 'keepers. Few men have better understood wicket-keepers and their problems. As for the other 'keeper, well, I remember Freddie Brown telling me many years ago that he thought the safest pair of hands in the country belonged to Keith Andrew, the former Northamptonshire 'keeper who toured Australia with me in 1954–55. Keith is now an MCC coach, travelling all over the country teaching the game, and is clearly a man very much involved with the game.

A captain must be knowledgeable in all facets of the game – wicket-keeping included – and the skipper I chose was Ted Dexter. I played in the Test against New Zealand at Old Trafford in 1958 when Ted made his debut and he scored an excellent half century. He was a marvellous clean hitter, never afraid to attack the quicker bowlers. Fred

Trueman accepted my invitation to join the panel as the representative of the fast bowling fraternity; and he has always been forthright with his views at our meetings. Jim Laker, the finest off-spinner I have seen, is another who says what he thinks. Jim bowled while I was behind the stumps so many times that he grew to appreciate all the nuances – strengths and weaknesses – of my game. The panel was completed by the recruitment of Reg Hayter, a journalist in Fleet Street for more than fifty years and proprietor of the premier sports reporting agency in Britain. He fully understands how to gain maximum exposure.

At our inaugural lunch, we discussed exactly what qualities we were looking for in potential award winners. We decided that a wicket-keeper's ability with the bat would be considered only if every facet of his game behind the stumps was equal to another player's. The Gordon's Gin award is essentially for wicket-keeping ability alone. We would take into consideration a 'keeper's ability both standing up and back; his gathering of returns and how quickly he gets up to the stumps; his performance on different types of wickets; his readiness to stand up to the medium-pacers; and his general enthusiasm and effect on the fielding performance of his team.

Each monthly winner – May to August inclusive – receives £500, of which £250 goes to the nominated player and the other £250 to the county he plays for. This allows the county to spend the money on, for example, coaching courses for young 'keepers on their staff or for equipment, so that youngsters making their way in the game should not have to dig too deeply into their own pockets. The annual award is £2,000 – split equally between player and county. So, players are clearly keen to win these awards, for the financial rewards if nothing else.

Derek Taylor, the Somerset wicket-keeper, now retired, whose haul in May 1982 included a world one-day record of eight in one innings, was our first monthly winner. The June award went to Bob Taylor, who kept superbly during the one-day internationals against India, and Bruce French, the young stumper from Nottinghamshire, was the next winner. French's consistency had been outstanding during

July and he proved his reputation as one of the best young 'keepers in the country. The August award went to Jack Richards, who performed splendidly during the latter part of the season, and Bob Taylor was the annual winner. Bob was the unanimous choice of the panel – he was superb for England and Derbyshire and the way he rallied his team-mates while fielding was an inspiration. His conduct both on and off the field was impeccable. An award-giving dinner was held at the Ritz in London, when Johnny Holbeach, managing director of Gordon's, presented Bob with his trophy. The first year was an unqualified success.

So to the 1983 season. May, a month when cricket was ravaged by the weather, signalled Alan Knott's first award. Although much of the programme was truncated by rain, Knotty still shone during the month. His handling and footwork on the often slippery grass were superb. David East of Essex, under strong challenge from Middlesex's Paul Downton, just prevailed in June. One feature of East's play was, as a left-hander, the number of diving catches he held with his right hand. East has made noticeable strides in the last couple of years and Essex's success in 1983 was as much to do with him as the more regularly-lauded exploits of Ken McEwan and John Lever. Chris Maynard of Lancashire won in July – the month in which he equalled the county record of six catches in an innings. Bob Taylor, French and David Bairstow (although David did not keep quite as well as in previous seasons, his willingness to stand up to the medium-pacers was commendable) challenged Maynard for the July award. Bobby Parks, the son of Jim, former Sussex and England player, was the beneficiary in August. Bobby's handling of Malcolm Marshall, the West Indian widely regarded as the fastest bowler in county cricket, and ability when standing up to brisk medium-pacer Tim Tremlett caught the eye, and David East of Essex (the County Championship winners and Benson and Hedges Cup runners-up) received the nod for the annual award. Sir Len Hutton was among the guests at the dinner at the Savoy, when Mr Holbeach again made the presentations.

Being chairman of the committee has allowed me to

travel all over the country watching cricket – keeping a particularly close eye, of course, on the performance of wicket-keepers. I bought an Autostrada, a type of home on wheels, allowing me to travel and stay overnight without difficulty. People see that I am actually monitoring the wicket-keeper's displays – and I know that all my fellow committeemen watch a lot of cricket.

The standard of wicket-keeping has risen dramatically over the last ten or twelve years – players are so much fitter for a start – and I believe incentives like the Gordon's Gin awards can only improve them still further. I know all the counties and players are grateful that the performances of the wicket-keepers are at last being recognised.

15

A Match of My Dreams

SELECTING IMAGINARY teams is one of most cricket lovers' favourite pastimes. Perhaps the finest eleven players available from one country or county; maybe a side made up exclusively from left-handed batsmen and left-arm bowlers. My two teams comprise the greatest players of my adult life – men I have played either with or against, or have subsequently admired from the stand – and will meet in a match of my dreams.

Much soul-searching was required before I finally arrived at my 22 players – or should I say 21, because I was going to make sure I played in a match of this quality! I suddenly realised how many great players I would have to leave out. I am sure a lot of people will dispute my selections, but I had a lot of fun coming up with the final choice.

The match, to be played at Lord's, is not to be taken too seriously. Nothing like a computer has been used to produce the outcome – just my imagination, which probably ran away from me a little at times. It is impossible to predict how players from one era would fare against those of another. But I enjoyed guessing and, hopefully, this imaginary match gives some idea of these great cricketers' particular qualities.

My Team

Sir Leonard Hutton   An automatic choice, Len possessed extraordinary talent allied to a marvellous temperament. He glided so many balls from the middle of his bat on either side of the wicket that people sometimes forget the power of his strokeplay. A Hutton cover drive was struck with great force.

Barry Richards A great opening batsman must be able to score rapidly against even the best bowling side – and Richards, the South African, could do just that. Therefore, he gets my vote ahead of players such as Arthur Morris and Geoffrey Boycott. Richards had a superb technique and all the shots. Unfortunately, politics prevented him from illustrating his ability for a prolonged period at Test level and, as a result, he occasionally seemed a little lethargic in his approach. A match of this nature would surely inspire him.

Sir Donald Bradman Nobody could argue with this choice. The most phenomenal of all run scorers. Concentration, technique and the will to make massive scores – coupled with his remarkable eye – enabled him to punish all bowling on almost all pitches. A fine fielder to boot. 'The Don' would also captain my side.

Wally Hammond I am not sure what Hammond, my vice-captain, would have thought about Bradman skippering the side ahead of him. The pair were adversaries for, including the War years, almost two decades. Hammond had a majesty about everything he did, with his broad shoulders and positive stride. Primarily a glorious batsman, he was also able to bowl medium-pacers that moved very late and he was a breathtaking, close-to-the-wicket fielder.

Denis Compton My dear old friend Denis, with a delightful mixture of flair, panache and cheek, was a genius with the bat. His bat looked wider than the stumps when he was in form.

Neil Harvey A little low in the order – but where else could he go? – comes this magnificent Australian. I was keen to include a left-hander among the specialist batsmen. Neil had an unflappable temperament. I recall Alec Bedser bowling to him in the early part of his career – Neil was only a young man – and he played and missed incessantly. Yet he was totally unperturbed and kept battling away. He had an extensive repertoire of strokes and was a magnificent cover fielder.

Sir Garfield Sobers Surely the greatest of all cricketers. A rapier-like left-handed batsman, who for a long time was the most prolific run scorer in Test cricket; a deceptively quick new-ball bowler, he could also swing an ageing ball both ways at a reduced pace and then bowl orthodox left-arm spin or even chinamen and googlies. Sobers was also a wonderful close fielder who even kept wicket. He was better than Miller, Botham, Procter and the rest. Probably also superior to Grace, Rhodes and Hirst, from another era.

Godfrey Evans I might feel a little humble in this company. But I could not resist the temptation on this once in a lifetime opportunity to play in this team. I would probably go in at about number eight.

Ray Lindwall A hostile and intelligent fast bowler. Lindwall's partnership with Keith Miller was a main reason for the success of Don Bradman's 1948 touring team. Ray was also a useful late-order batsman, although this facet of his game would scarcely be required in a side of this batting strength.

Jim Laker The finest off-spinner I have seen. Jim is, of course, remembered mainly for his nineteen wickets for 90 at Old Trafford in 1956, but that one remarkable performance should never be allowed to mask the fact that he was a great off-break bowler throughout the fifties. That was merely the highlight of a superb career.

Freddie Trueman Fred had real pace at the start of his career. He reduced his speed slightly later on, but with no loss of effect; he had cunning, ability to move the ball, and a clever change of pace. Everyone of Fred's deliveries was bowled with that magnificently fluent action.

Not a bad side, I think you will agree! Four of the batsmen scored more than one hundred hundreds and doubtless

Richards, Harvey and Sobers would have done if they had played longer and more frequently. Lindwall, Trueman and Sobers provide the speed; Hammond and Sobers the swing, seam and medium-pace; Laker, Sobers and, if necessary, Compton – who could bowl useful left-arm leg-breaks – the spin. The fielding would be first-rate. Michael Holding, a genuinely fast bowler with a lovely action, is my twelfth man.

The Opposition

Gordon Greenidge   I was keen to choose a player capable of taking an attack apart to open the innings. Greenidge can do so, although occasionally his desire to get on top of the bowling from the start proves his undoing.

Arthur Morris   Geoffrey Boycott, Colin McDonald and Bobby Simpson pushed Arthur close as contenders for the other opener's place. But the left-handed Australian got my vote largely because of his temperament. Only when Alec Bedser discovered a weakness in the Morris armour – the inswinging delivery that often penetrated his defence – did he appear anything other than almost impossible to dislodge.

Vivian Richards   In the Denis Compton mould – an instinctive genius with the bat. Viv has a measure of arrogance at the wicket, where he looks to be in total command, hits the ball very hard indeed and is especially strong on the legside.

Graeme Pollock   Pollock often reminded those fortunate enough to have seen them both of Frank Woolley. They share the same philosophy – hit the ball hard, high and often – and, of course, they were both left-handers. Pollock was the best left-handed batsman of his generation.

Clyde Walcott   I just had to include one of the three 'Ws' and Walcott received my vote because of his enormous power, even against the fastest bowlers. He was especially strong off the back foot and, at one time, was probably a slightly superior player to either Worrell or Weekes.

Keith Miller Keith would captain the opposition – his devil-may-care attitude had the knack of bringing the best out of people. He also had an acute tactical aware-ness, as he showed when skippering New South Wales to victory over MCC in 1954–55 – our only defeat outside the Tests on that tour. He was a very fast bowler when he so wished and a magnificent attacking batsman. Perhaps he did not make as many runs as his talent deserved. Keith was not unknown to allow his concentration to waver when there were plenty of runs on the board – and, anyway, he might have fancied a rest if the racing was on television!

Ian Botham Ian can win matches with either bat or ball. I have always believed his batting to be superior, although nobody can argue with his remarkable bowling achieve-ments. He could easily become the greatest wicket-taker in Test history.

Don Tallon I do not believe I have seen a better wicket-keeper than Don Tallon. He was quite supreme. Other 'keepers – such as Rod Marsh and Alan Knott – have had more run-scoring potential, but I have always main-tained that the best wicket-keeper should be picked. If he can bat, it is an added bonus.

Frank Tyson Tyson was the fastest bowler I have seen. On the tour to Australia in 1954–55 he was bowling like the wind off a shortened run. We must assume that all the players are performing to the peak of their powers in this match, and on that tour Tyson was devastating.

Dennis Lillee The record wicket-taker in Test cricket, Dennis was very fast indeed when he first burst on to the international scene at the start of the seventies. Rather like Fred Trueman, he reduced his pace slightly, but still ran through the best batting sides. Lillee has overcome a terrible back injury that would have ruined the careers of lesser men. He makes no secret of his dislike of batsmen and nobody can ever question his determination.

Sonny Ramadhin   Sonny got more top-class batsmen into difficulty than just about any spinner I can remember. When he came over to England in 1950, we all had enormous problems trying to spot his variations of spin. I would like to include Doug Wright, a real match-winner, but he was too prone to inconsistency.

Clive Lloyd, as much for his fielding as for his batting, would be Keith Miller's twelfth man. I remember playing for the International Cavaliers one Sunday in Birmingham in a benefit match for Tom Cartwright. The batsman hammered a juicy half-volley towards extra-cover. I dashed up towards the stumps just in case and the batsman moved a few strides down the pitch, admiring his apparently certain boundary. But he did not account for big Clive. Moving round from cover point, Lloyd dived full length and stopped the ball with his outstretched right hand. Then, from a sitting position, Clive flung the ball to me – it never reached more than six feet off the ground – and I, reaching the stumps just in time, whipped off the bails. The batsman's frantic efforts to recover his ground were in vain and he was run out by two feet.

The Match

The ground was bathed in sunshine, with a slight breeze blowing from the Pavilion End, and the Lord's pitch looked a good one – it needed to be to last six days. Don Bradman called correctly and had little hesitation in deciding to bat.

Len Hutton, opening with Barry Richards, was in good form and played three imperious cover drives off Frank Tyson, who was given the benefit of the wind ahead of his new-ball partner Dennis Lillee. Then Keith Miller brought himself on first change and whipped one back; the ball caught the inside edge of Hutton's bat and Don Tallon took a magnificent tumbling catch down the legside.

The crowd hushed in anticipation of another monumental innings from Bradman. And he did not disappoint them. Richards was the dominant partner, though, in their stand. He batted beautifully, providing a graphic illustration of how politics had deprived him from showing his talents to a worldwide audience, and looked set for a century until he misjudged Sonny Ramadhin's flighted leg break. Richards edged an attempted drive and Ian Botham held a straightforward catch at slip.

Bradman by now was moving into his stride, offering the bowlers scarcely a semblance of hope. He reached his century shortly before tea and it came as some surprise when he missed a straight one from Tyson. Bradman's innings of 145 included 19 boundaries. Tyson, suitably inspired by dismissing Bradman, went through Wally Hammond for pace, but not before my team's vice-captain had scored 72, including an enormous six into the Grandstand off Ramadhin.

Denis Compton, despite the solid foundation laid by the first four batsmen, struggled. Indeed, he often needed a challenge to bring the best out of him. I recall the match at The Oval in 1938, when England scored 903 for seven against Australia and Hutton contributed 364. England reached 546 before the third wicket fell and Eddie Paynter, due to go in number five, bet Compton, the number six, that they would not score ten runs between them. Watching Hutton, Maurice Leyland and Wally Hammond piling on the runs, Denis accepted the wager with alacrity. Paynter was lbw bowled O'Reilly for 0 and Compton bowled Waite for 1. Mervyn Waite played only two Test matches for Australia, and his figures were one for 190. Not a bad scalp, though, for his only Test wicket, and he always buys Denis a drink when they meet.

Compton, having already been dropped once, was snapped up by Miller off Lillee. Neil Harvey prospered briefly before Botham 'tucked' him up with an in-ducker, the ball went in the air off bat and pad and Tallon, diving forward, took an improbable catch. Garfield Sobers seized command immediately, but Miller, with a gambling piece of captaincy, summoned Viv Richards to bowl. Richards was likely either to be punished, or take a wicket as the batsmen sought to attack his gentle seamers. The latter happened as

Sobers, with his first indiscretion, lifted his head in an attempt to hit the ball out the ground and missed. Sobers, dismissed for 60, was eighth out. In the meantime, I had walked fearlessly to the wicket to replace Harvey – and walked straight back again, bowled by Miller first ball. I hardly even saw it!.

Our tail did not last long and we were all out for 465 – a large score, but nonetheless we were still left with a feeling of what might have been. Only Bradman, inevitably, had made a truly major score, while most of the other batsmen did the hard bit by becoming established and then getting out.

Gordon Greenidge, in his usual pugnacious way, quickly looked to gain the initiative when the opposition went in, shortly after lunch on the second day. The Hampshire opener twice hooked Fred Trueman to the fence, but canny old Fred gained his revenge.

He moved a couple away from Greenidge, at which he played and missed, and then brought one back and trapped Greenidge leg before. Viv Richards joined Morris and, with the pitch probably now at its peak for batting, they added 124 for the second wicket. Morris, the more pedestrian of the two, attempted to escape from his shackles by driving at Jim Laker. The ball turned sharply for the first time in the match, Morris got an edge and I held the catch. I was particularly pleased, because no catch is easy standing up.

Richards and Graeme Pollock, two masters of the modern generation, were joined and their liaison produced the most exciting batting of the game so far. Their stand of 68 occupied just 43 minutes before Richards, driving lazily at Ray Lindwall, dragged the ball on. His innings of 112 included two sixes and 16 fours.

Miller's brief stay ended when he was bowled by Trueman and then Pollock, hitting against the gradually increasing spin being extracted by Laker, was caught from a skier by Harvey in the covers. Botham was as belligerent as ever, twice hitting Laker for straight sixes, until Sobers, bowling orthodox slow left-arm, lured him out of his ground and I completed the stumping.

A Match of My Dreams

By now, Walcott was hitting the ball with thunderous power – one feature of the game, despite its importance, had been the willingness of players to bat in attacking fashion. Clyde was trying to manipulate the strike as much as possible but, in an effort to take a single from the last ball of an over, Don Tallon, his partner, was run out by Harvey's direct hit from cover. Lindwall and Trueman ran through the tail, leaving Walcott just sufficient time to complete a magnificent century. My team led by a mere eleven runs on first innings. The game could hardly have been more finely balanced.

The opposition had scored their runs at a good rate and were all out half an hour before the close on the third day. This left Hutton and Richards an awkward 20 minutes to negotiate, which they did in the face of a hostile onslaught from Tyson and Lillee.

The pitch still looked a good one after the rest day, but Richards soon misjudged the line and was bowled by Lillee during an aggressive spell by the Australian fast bowler on the fourth morning. Bradman cracked a couple of boundaries and again looked ominous before Lillee, by now inspired, made one nip back and Walcott picked up a smart catch off bat and pad at short leg.

Hutton progressed steadily while Hammond, again reeling off a succession of fluent offside strokes, overtook Hutton before having his middle stump extracted by Miller. Hammond's 68, scored in under two hours, included a dozen boundaries. Compton, eager to make up for his first innings failure, joined Hutton and this pair took root.

Hutton, nudging, pushing and deflecting and occasionally unleashing a glorious shot through the covers, reached a four-hour century before mistiming a drive straight to Pollock at mid-on. He and Compton added 103 for the fourth wicket and, by now, Denis was at his intuitive best. A capacity crowd, basking in continuous sunshine, revelled in a Compton special. The famous sweep was working well – always a sign of Compton at his best – and just about every other shot in the book. He and Harvey, who prospered briefly, put on 56 and Sobers helped add 47. I joined Compton, never the world's safest runner, and he was run out by Miller's brilliant pick up and direct hit from square leg. Compton's 134, possibly the innings of the match, was chanceless and took three-and-a-half hours to compile.

Lindwall, after three fours off the middle of the bat, was yorked by Botham. Laker, who snicked his first ball for four, was trapped leg before by Botham's break-back from his second. Trueman was caught at second slip and I, much to my relief following my first-ball departure in the first innings, remained 20 not out.

We were all out for 434, leaving the opposition 446 to win. No side in Test match history had ever scored so many to win; but the pitch was still playing well although, with the odd bare patch appearing, the bounce was becoming a little variable.

Although the match had produced some heavy scoring, few people in the crowd truly believed the opposition could reach their target as Greenidge and Morris walked out to open their second innings. They shared a partnership of 68 before Morris fell to a smart slip catch by Hutton. Those modern West Indies masters, Greenidge and Viv Richards, were separated when Greenidge attempted an extravagant square slash off Laker and I held the snick standing up.

Richards and Pollock, employing attacking methods, attempted to get right on top of the bowling. It succeeded until Richards, looking to hit a ball from Laker somewhere in the direction of St John's Wood underground station, mistimed and was caught by Compton on the mid-wicket boundary.

Walcott, fresh from his first innings century, joined Pollock and the pair struck the ball fiercely. Walcott, intermingling powerful drives off the back foot with blows over mid-wicket, scored 45 before succumbing lbw to one from Sobers that kept low. Pollock went on.

The South African, surviving a sharp caught and bowled chance offered to Laker when 71, had reached 119 when, expecting a chinaman, he was completely bamboozled by Sobers and clean bowled. Pollock hit 14 fours and 3 sixes – one a remarkable shot over extra-cover off Trueman. Somehow, I don't think Fred enjoyed that! Miller and Botham, coming together at 312 for five, took the score beyond 400 and it looked odds-on that the opposition were about to pull off a remarkable victory. Then Botham, having hooked a Lindwall bouncer for six two balls earlier, did not quite get to the pitch of a mighty drive and Bradman took a stinging catch in the covers. The onus was now very much on captain Keith Miller. He did not let his team down.

Tallon, running sharply between the wickets, reached double figures before Trueman got him leg before and it was 428 for seven. Now, with Miller already past fifty, the opposition again looked favourites to win. Tyson edged a four and scampered two singles before Lindwall beat him for pace. Lillee was yorked second ball and that brought Lindwall's fruitful over to an end.

The score was 437 for nine and the tension was almost unbearable as Trueman began the next over. Miller struck the second delivery for four over mid-off and he and Ramadhin ran two from the third ball. The field closed in for the fifth ball but Miller, dropping the ball at his feet, saw an opportunity for a single and ran. He and Ramadhin made it. Two needed for victory and one wicket standing.

Trueman, sensing it could be his last ball of this historic match, summoned one final effort. The ball pitched on off stump and moved sufficiently to coax an edge. I saw it clearly as I moved to my right but, inexplicably, the ball struck my right glove flush on the palm and bounced out, but upwards rather than downwards. Time stood still. A split second seemed like an eternity. I caught it. My fumble, my juggle, my catch gave my team victory by one run in a remarkable game of cricket. Miller was stranded 83 not out.

Nobody can state with real certainty how players from different generations would fare against each other. So this match is largely make-believe. But it is fun wondering whether Bradman would score so many runs against the batteries of fast bowlers that proliferate today. Or would Lindwall have quite the same success against, say, Viv and

THE SCOREBOARD

My Team

L.Hutton, c Tallon, b Miller	36	c Pollock, b Ramadhin	105
B.A.Richards, c Botham, b Ramadhin	75	b Lillee	21
*D.G.Bradman, b Tyson	145	c Walcott, b Lillee	10
W.R.Hammond, b Tyson	72	b Miller	68
D.C.S.Compton, c Miller, b Lillee	16	run out	134
R.N.Harvey, c Tallon, b Botham	32	c Tallon, b Tyson	25
G.S.Sobers, b Richards	60	c Botham, b Ramadhin	19
†T.G.Evans, b Miller	0	not out	20
R.R.Lindwall, c Botham, b Tyson	5	b Botham	12
J.C.Laker, c Botham, b Lillee	3	lbw b Botham	4
F.S.Trueman, not out	8	c Miller, b Lillee	3
Extras	13	Extras	13
Total	465	Total	434

Bowling: Tyson 26–6–78–3; Lillee 22.5–4–69–2; Miller 16–3–74–2; Botham 29–10–99–1; Ramadhin 42–14–102–1; Richards 8–2–30–1.
Second Innings: Lillee 36.1–14–60–3; Tyson 21–5–88–1; Ramadhin 37–10–113–2; Miller 18–7–54–1; Botham 18–4–84–2; Richards 6–2–12–0; Walcott 3–0–10–0.

The Opposition

C.G.Greenidge, lbw b Trueman	19	c Evans, b Laker	54
A.R.Morris, c Evans, b Laker	60	c Hutton b Trueman	32
I.V.A.Richards, b Lindwall	112	c Compton, b Laker	42
R.G.Pollock, c Harvey, b Laker	72	b Sobers	119
C.L.Walcott, not out	102	lbw b Sobers	45
*K.R.Miller, b Trueman	14	not out	83
I.T.Botham, st Evans, b Sobers	37	c Bradman, b Lindwall	41
†D.Tallon, run out	2	lbw b Trueman	10
F.H.Tyson, b Lindwall	14	b Lindwall	6
D.K.Lillee, c Bradman, b Lindwall	6	b Lindwall	0
S.Ramadhin, b Trueman	0	c Evans, b Trueman	0
Extras	16	Extras	12
Total	454	Total	444

Bowling: Lindwall 27–12–59–3; Trueman 19.4–5–83–3; Sobers 22–6–89–1; Laker 46–14–139–2; Hammond 14–4–42–0; Compton 7–1–26–0.
Second Innings: Lindwall 20–6–66–3; Trueman 24–8–79–3; Laker 47–16–114–2; Hammond 5–2–9–0; Sobers 30–8–94–2; Compton 19–5–70–0.

* captain   † wicket-keeper

Barry Richards? My feeling is that the outstanding players from one era would, if born at another time, adapt to the particular demands of any generation. They would still be exceptional cricketers.

Selecting world elevens is an almost impossible task. I am sure you could ask a hundred people, and none of them would come up with exactly the same two teams as mine. Here, then, in no particular order, are some of the players I was reluctantly forced to leave out: Frank Worrell, Everton Weekes, Ted Dexter, Alan Knott, Ian and Greg Chappell, Rodney Marsh, Rohan Kanhai, Alec Bedser, Peter May, Basil d'Oliveira, Colin Cowdrey, Geoff Boycott, Wes Hall, Charlie Griffith, Andy Roberts, Bobby Simpson, Colin McDonald, Joel Garner, Alan Davidson, Richie Benaud, Norman O'Neill, Sid Barnes, Tom Graveney, Trevor Bailey, David Gower, John Snow, Mike Procter, Tony Lock, Johnny Wardle, Hugh Tayfield, Glenn Turner, Martin Donnelly, Kenny Barrington, Bill and John Edrich, Alvin Kallicharran, Sunil Gavaskar, Kapil Dev, Hanif Mohammad, Zaheer Abbas, Javed Miandad, Richard Hadlee, Derek Underwood, Bob Willis, Brian Statham, Graham McKenzie, Lance Gibbs, Bishen Bedi, Venkat, Chandrasekhar, Prasanna, Imran Khan, Jeff Thomson, Bob Taylor – etc., etc. One could pick half a dozen other teams whose strength would be hardly less than my two.

The atmosphere in the dressing-room, of course, was marvellous. The great players in my fictitious match span more than 50 years of cricket at the highest level. The anecdotes were certainly flowing. I recalled the time when, in Sydney in 1946–47, Sid Barnes and Bradman put on 405 for the fifth wicket. On the Saturday evening, Barnes appealed against the bad light after every ball and eventually the umpires granted his wish, by which time the sun was actually shining. Incidentally, batsmen were prohibited from appealing between each delivery after that.

It also rained and, in those days in Australia, the pitch was rolled if damaged by rain. By Monday morning, it was an absolute beauty, bound together by the rain and now bone dry. Bradman, who had kept himself back overnight, went on the rampage, before eventually being dismissed for 234. Sid turned to me and said: 'Nobody's going to remember me if I score more than Bradman. And even less so if I got less than him. I think the answer is to get out for 234.' Without addition to the Australian score, Barnes was caught Ikin, bowled Bedser for 234. I cannot imagine many batsmen have got themselves out on purpose in Test cricket. Australia won the match by an innings and 33 runs. I remember Len Hutton turning to me after we had bowled another unproductive over in the grilling heat and saying: 'You know, Godfrey, there's nowt for it, but run t'buggers out!'

Ray Lindwall recounted the occasion, during the Old Trafford Test of 1948, when Bill Edrich, who could be decidedly quick with his slinging action, sent down three bouncers in one over at Ray. The third of them pinched Ray's hand against the bat handle. He flung his bat down and removed his glove; we gathered round asking if he was all right and whether he would like to go off for a while. Edrich said: 'Are you okay, Lindy?' Lindwall replied: 'You can't do this to me and get away with it. And, no, I'm not going off.' Of course, when Bill batted, Lindwall sent down a whole stream of bumpers. But it did not worry Bill much. He was one of the toughest campaigners in the business and stood up to it all. We all had a laugh and drink about it later. Bill was a very gritty player and I have always been surprised that he didn't play more than 39 Tests for England. He should certainly have been on the 1950–51 tour to Australia.